Wh
Category Management

Mark Taylor

Mark Taylor

ISBN-13:
978-1494459130

ISBN-10:
1494459132

DEDICATION

Thanks to all of my family, friends and colleagues who have added value to my life and taught me enough to need to empty my head onto these pages.

Mark Taylor

CONTENTS

	Acknowledgments	i
1	The crime scene	1
2	Motives for Murder	8
3	Retailer vs Manufacturer	17
4	Category Management in Retail	29
5	Category Management in Manufacturers	34
6	Welcome to the Game	45
7	Signs of life	54
8	Retail Shopper Management	66
9	Shopper and Consumer Metrics	87
10	Who Killed Category Management?	103

Mark Taylor

ACKNOWLEDGMENTS

Special thanks to Dr Dan Herman, Dr Andy Boynton, and Dr John J. Medina. for allowing me to include some of their ideas in this book.

1 THE CRIME SCENE

Category Management lies in a pool of its own blood. The heat is seeping out of its body and its pulse is fading fast. On its face a fixed stare. It knows something has happened but it does not know what. It is about to become a statistic of the unforgiving business world we live in.

The violence with which the attack has happened is beyond its understanding and because of this is does not know how to react. It is lost.

Many people who knew and loved Category Management will not believe it has been cut down in its prime and, like the rumours about Elvis`death, they will assume it's a lie.

But it`s not. The body is cold on the hard ground and the only thing left to do is bury it before it stinks the place up.

But we can`t leave it like this can we? Category Management served us well for so many years, the least we can do is to discover who committed this atrocity and what were their motives.

Over the course of this book I ask you to help me answer some tough questions to reveal the truth about this crime.

Let me be very clear at this point, Category Management had many beautiful, sound processes and attributes that made it a great tool in the hands of common sense professionals.

Yes it could be unwieldy at times and often needed to be simplified to make it manageable in everyday life but it did provide significant value to retail businesses around the world.

It was also evolving at exponential rates due to technological advances in data management and analysis which, combined with new thinking about how to describe consumer and shopper clusters, delivered real world Return On Investment (ROI).

For now lets assume it is still alive and try to work out what anyone could have against it.

It has become part of the retail structure and accepted as best practice by many.

Consultancies around the world make big bucks training it and, for some people reading this book, it is in the title of their job. Lots of reasons for it to be kept alive.

But it`s not all perfect.

Here is one place where someone could have a problem with it. Category Management is theoretically the answer to the question "How can I best satisfy a shoppers/consumers needs and make money in the process?"

The idea sounds simple enough. If I as a retailer understand my customers behaviour, shopping habits, product preferences, personal drivers well enough and I meet these needs within my store then I will have a competitive point of difference and the theory works.

Over more than 20 years Category Management has been used to evolve the retail environment into its current incarnation. It is reasonable to assume that after this period of time we must be getting close to what great looks like.

Voltaire said "Judge a man by his questions rather than by his answers."

So here is the first question I have in my investigators mind. If Category Management is the answer to the challenge of meeting shoppers needs and delivering a competitive point of differentiation for retailers to maximise profit, then why are we living in a retail landscape of "me too" stores delivering dull, boring, unimaginative and sometimes depressing environments to shop in?

Yes that is very harsh isn't it. To find the perpetrator we have be ruthless in our pursuit of the truth and this will hurt feelings sometimes.

Anyway, how can I say boring with the abundance of different formats, ranges, pricing structures, layouts and retail brands in the world?

If you have come across Ockham`s Razor this will make perfect sense.

The principle states that "among competing hypotheses, the hypothesis with the fewest assumptions should be selected". The simplest theory to explain an observed result is often the correct one.

So if Category Management is working just dandy for everyone why is it that your children do not wake up on a Saturday morning and come running into your bedroom begging to go grocery shopping.

In your head do you say "This is a great day, I get to spend the next 2 hours of my life going to the supermarket " or do you say "I have to drag myself grocery shopping on a Saturday rather than do something I enjoy, where did my life go so wrong?"

Do you think "I have to go grocery shopping" or "I want to go grocery shopping"?

Now a simple come back is that people often enjoy shopping. Yes they do. I enjoy shopping mostly but what is it they enjoy. Is it the ownership or use of the product or the experience of shopping for it. They are completely different.

Do I get "excited" owning a new car? Yes. Do I get "excited" dealing with car salesmen? No, not really in most instances.

Do I "enjoy" cooking a meal from scratch? Yes. Do I "enjoy" fighting for a car parking space and standing in a queue in the mall at the weekend to buy the produce? No, not really.

Am I "happy" to put on some new clothes to go out to dinner with friends? Yes (depending on the friends of course). Am I "happy" to hunt for my size in a disorganised pile of jeans, wait for a changing room and then try on clothes in near tropical temperatures? No, I would rather hit my head with a hammer for an hour if thats ok.

Category Management is not taking into consideration higher needs that shoppers have in the modern, fast paced world we live in. It is purely providing retailers and manufacturers a "ticket to the show". What does this mean?

As a shopper and consumer a person has certain expectations from a retail store and the products they buy in them.

They should have the product on the shelves. Certainly core and staples at least. No out of stocks.
Ranges should have width and depth to be credible.
Product should not be damaged in any way and first quality.
They expect it to be competitively priced.
The pricing should be clear and easy to see.
There should be good promotions on core and extended range products.
Stores should be clean and tidy.
Each shop should be easy to navigate and all categories "shoppable" (no impediments to getting to the product).
Queues should not exist at the till.
Customer service should be excellent.
The process should leave them with a positive customer experience.

All of these are a given before they will part with their hard earned cash. Let them down on any of these and they will vote with their feet and take their business to the next best alternative.

Achieving this is the bare minimum a retailer has to do to be in the game. It is interesting that many retailers look like they believe this is the final solution rather than the starting point.

The battle for share of pocket is now at fever pitch with new emerging must have products appearing continuously.

Think about it in these terms. If you stand in your average, local, grocery superstore and look around could you be in one of a dozen different retailers with the biggest point of difference being the colour scheme. Maybe the coffee shop has different flavour muffins, or better class of tables depending which market sector it believes it appeals to. It may even have a well known restaurant franchise in it but to all intents and purposes the store itself is basically the same. Same brands, same offers and same delivery.

It will have fresh vegetables, meats, bread, dairy, fish counter, hot food, deli, home consumables clothes etc. Maybe a dry cleaners or some other convenient added value proposition to the store but what else?

Why do you think that even the biggest and most profitable retailers in the world can lose significant market share to competitors in days if they get their peak trading plans wrong? It's simple, they are too interchangeable and have no significant point of difference that creates "Destination". Another contentious challenge, this time about being "Destination". We will come back to this later.

In a mall environment, which may cater to shoppers wider needs, you only need to step from the walkways into a store and you are back to the same proposition again, often with the real excitement being delivered by the prospect of ownership of the product, not the experience of obtaining it.

Now this does not mean there aren't any great places to shop which are completely different from this but lets be realistic. What percentage of the retail landscape do these exceptions make up? How many Apple stores are there compared to out of town electrical? How many Abercrombie & Fitch verses traditional clothing stores? How many Bass Pro Shops (mentioned later in the book) can be stacked against a sea of Hyper Markets sporting goods sections?

When a consumer goes grocery shopping they do not just give up on Maslow's hierarchy of needs just because they want good pricing and product that is in date.

Shoppers and consumers have evolved significantly over the last 20 years. Their lives are richer, more vibrant and experiential than before. They expect more from life and not just in materialistic ways. They also expect more for and from themselves personally. Many of them want to be fulfilled not just secure. To be happy not just content. To be excited not just safe.

Fulfilling customer needs is at a higher level now.

As an example lets look at how telephones have changed during that period. They used to be about enabling people to keep in touch for business and personal reasons while separated by distance. In 20 years (about the time category management has been around) they have evolved through several of Maslow's levels. They have helped satisfy the need for social status, entertainment and emotional fulfilment. They have kept pace with the changing needs of the consumer and, as a result, people like Steve Jobs have revolutionised the place a telephone occupies in our lives.

Has Category Management been responsible for this? No! Has it helped the FMCG retail and manufacturing sector match our growing need for self actualisation and our higher expectations for emotional fulfilment? No and it has failed to do some more fundamental things too.

During recent years I hear retailers and manufacturers strive to deliver image and excitement for shoppers and consumers. In the last 100 shopping trips you made how often did you feel excited by the experience? Genuinely excited. Christmas morning for a 5 year old excited! Exactly.

So what or who is the problem? Is it Category Management itself that causes the issue?

These are key questions but more importantly how can we retain the great deliverables that Category Management has achieved while realising retails promise to "satisfy a shopper or consumers needs".

Over the next few chapters we will explore the reasons behind the problem, deal with the reality of everyday business pressures and breathe some new life into a stagnant environment. We may even find the shocking truth about the murderer. Is it a conspiracy? Could there be dangers for others in the future. Could one of those at risk be you?

We will also try to discover what part Retail Shopper Management will play in the sad demise of Category Management.

This Who-done-it is not about a consultancy selling their spin on why the future of the world has to involve purchasing their services (although please don't let this stop you hiring me to help your business if you really want to). It is, in fact, a challenge to retailers and manufacturers to live up to the modern demands of a Joe or Jane in the street, to make their life better, more fun and more fulfilling. Not just cheaper.

2 MOTIVES FOR MURDER
OR
"LIES, DAMN LIES AND CATEGORY MANAGEMENT!"

The time is January 2006 and I had just taken the Buying and Merchandising Directors position at a large, but failing, UK electrical retailer.

In the first few weeks meetings had been arranged with our suppliers that included many of the worlds largest technology manufacturers. The objective was to find ways of adding value to our business and taking costs out.

After the initial meetings took place it became apparent that the sole objective of every supplier was to maintain the maximum number of SKUs from their range, which we stocked in our business, and if possible increase them.

In many ways I could understand some of this. As an ex Sales Manager myself I knew only too well the drive to achieve last years numbers plus the inevitable annual increase.

What stunned me, however, was that the requirement to add profit for my company as well as the manufacturer was often completely ignored.

Most proposals were presented in a very enthusiastic way but turned out to be sales increases for them at the expense of their competitors. Many of them actually suppressed our margins and reduced profit due to down trading. At best they made misguided assumptions such as market share equating to possible sales rates. e.g. "we have an

18% share of market and we only account for 10% of your range. If you increase our products listed you can increase sales by 8% immediately."

The "fair share" argument often preceded assumptions that their brand loyalty was 100% and that we were not driving their competitors products hard. In a largely substitutional market customers can be switched between big brands, and in-store conversion increased, by using "category killer deals" on competitors products.

As a buyer the "fair share" comment often sounds like a whiny kid begging for more and shows a lack of retail comprehension. "We are one of the biggest brands in the world and you are not giving us fair share of space" sounds more like "It's not fair, the other children get more sweets than me" to professional retail buyers.

Even in an advanced environment when share is attributed to the local market around a specific store (micro marketing) it still makes little sense if you are redefining the market as opposed to following it.

Needless to say these meetings ended up in a dogfight negotiation purely about price.

After several weeks of this we had some light at the end of the tunnel. A supplier in the vacuum cleaner category rang and told us they had finished a significant Category Management evaluation of the sector and could they share some of the results?

Of course they could! Perhaps a sensible opportunity gap could be highlighted and both companies could increase profits.

The day of the meeting arrives and so does the Sales Director to deliver the news.

He held out his hand and smiled broadly as he entered the office. "Good morning, how are you?" He said.

"Fine thank you and you? I replied.

"Excellent thanks." He said. "I have some fantastic news about the results of the Category Management work we have been undertaking."

"Really? Show me what you have for me." I replied with a certain apprehension.

"Well" he said "what we have found is that in the premium section of this sub category you are under-ranged. This is based on a comparison to other similar categories."

"You currently use the category as a Traffic Driver and we believe you should re define it as a Profit Driver" he continued. "In fact there is an opportunity to increase sales by 3% across the category as long as you re allocate space from the value and value plus products to the premium."

We ran through the comparison of shopper profiles and behaviour. Evaluated the difference and impact it would have on sales rates and I overlaid it with probable margins. Yes on paper it looked like we could change the definition and move sales forward.

I asked him for recommendations for new products from his range and told him I would follow it through with the Category Manager and let him know what our decision was.

During the next two weeks a proposal was put together for the reduction of the value and value plus end of the range and an extension to the premium products.

One of the items that was a suggested casualty of downsizing the value products was a little vacuum cleaner called Henry. No I am not joking. A Henry is a little round, red chappy with what looks like a bowler hat on top. He also has eyes and a smile.

A fun product that had a solid sale rate but low price and low margin.   Henry was also having a few problems because we had occasionally experienced some higher levels of returns, from customers, back to stores. On paper it looked like the little guy could be on his way out based on his scoring. He did not share basket with many other products although you would occasionally see him bought along with fridges,cookers,washing machines and dishwashers all in one till ring.

During this period I had the chance to work with my then CEO Chris Onslow. Chris is a graduate of Sir Philip Green`s retail empire and embodies some of the best practices any
manger in FMCG retail can adopt. He's a polarising person. You either love him or he drives you crazy with his energy, drive and demanding standards. However he affects you he will change your life and make you think smarter about retail. He changed my view of the world around me and instilled some disciplines I still adhere to today.

One of the most simple but significant initiatives Chris drove through the senior management team was that we spent as much time in store as we could. He knew that the problem with many retailers was that they allowed themselves to drift away from the shop floor, the place where the battle for shopper conversion takes place.

This meant most Saturdays and Sundays were spent visiting stores all over the country and talking to managers, staff and even more importantly shoppers.

On one visit I had the opportunity to discuss the proposed changes to the vacuum category with one of the customer retail team.

"What`s the story with the Henry?" I asked. "Seems like he could be on his way out".

"Not very reliable" says the nice lady looking after the section. "We have had several come back due to problems".

"Yes so I understand" I said. "So no problem if we decide to replace it with something else?" I asked.

"No, it would great. I wouldn't have so many builders bringing returns to store. They can be a pain." She said.

"Builders?" I asked. "Tell me about builders".

And so here the true story unfolds. The reason for the higher returns rate was that builders were buying Henry because he was basically bullet proof compared to many rivals. So much so he was being used to suck up rubble and construction dust on commercial sites!

His ability to digest debris was impressive and his price point meant he was great value. In fact he was a rock star in the world of vacuum cleaners!

But here is the kicker. Because builders were walking through our doors and seeing us as the point of purchase for electrical products they came back when they were fitting out houses and apartments.

Kill Henry from our range and we would effectively be de-listing many small builders from our stores. Along with builders you could include hoteliers who brought similar additional purchases when they were buying Henry for commercial purposes.

These were some of our most profitable customers. Not for this category but for the store.

A category manager could easily have made the right decision for the category profitability but the wrong choice for the rest of the chain. It would actually have reduced the sales in most other departments.

This is the first time I realised the limitations of classic Category Management. Since then the process has evolved and in some businesses these product changes are now validated by a wider audiences as a safeguard against this type of thing happening.

This practice is not common place though and relies on in-depth knowledge of the shopper. Not just as a sub group but also as an individual.

Categories run as individual business units, which is part of the core principles of Category Management, do not view the consumer from a wide enough perspective.

The introduction of a role in retailers designed to manage shoppers from a higher level is a move in the right direction but it still leaves a broken process which is being band-aided to work.

When you look at the retail landscape you only have to turn the next corner to see a successful example of a business that meets the higher needs of consumers and makes ridiculous amounts of cash in the process. Lets look at Starbucks for a minute.

Love them or hate them, it is impossible not to be impressed with their ability to grow and make money across the globe.

Their success, however, is not attributed to the quality of the coffee alone. The variety of cake options is not the sole reason for customers to flock to their doors. Food and drink are at the bottom of Maslow's pyramid but satisfying these fundamental needs is not what makes Starbucks popular.

Think about this for a moment, when you say to someone "let's go for a coffee" how often do you mean I am thirsty?

You may mean many different things:
"I'm tired of shopping I need to rest for a while"
"I want to talk to you to try to build a relationship one on one"
"I have to give you some bad feedback but want it to be less formal than a meeting"

A friend of mine has warned me to be more careful asking a girl for a coffee. In England it might mean "let's catch up" or even "let's talk and see where the evening goes". In some Mediterranean countries it can be more overt and if a girl says yes to coffee she may be talking about the one for breakfast the next morning. Personally this has never happened to me. I have obviously been going to the wrong Mediterranean countries.

This is also less likely to be the case for Starbucks customers, unless the chain begins opening hotels, so customers choose to visit for different reasons.

Actually Starbucks is about Love & Belonging. When Howard Schultz set the aspiration for his chain of coffee houses to become "The third place" (a safe, social place between
home and work) it was directed at meeting a persons need for friendship, intimacy, family and belonging. Starbucks is a community based opportunity to meet, converse and share.

The layout, furniture and feel of each location is designed to create an environment which is a comfortable place to socialise, work or relax. Oh and you can buy something to eat and drink if you want to while you are there.

If it was just about coffee, cake and low prices, people would take a flask and a packed lunch.

A competitive edge in this instance is partly delivered by satisfying deep felt needs of consumers which are far more marketable than purely satisfying a fundamental and low
level need to drink and eat. And to quote my old CEO at Fruit of the Loom, Bill Farley "If you haven't got a competitive edge, don't try to compete".

Category Management is, at best, delivering a credible point of purchase in the majority of retail stores. Geographically distressed purchases (eg grocery shopping close to where you live or work) allows stores which are just good enough to make money. But is this going to be enough in the future?

If all retailers stay the same then yes. But, realistically, what are the chances of retailing staying stagnant with pressure from internet sales and technological advances such as 3D printing (the ability for a product to be fabricated in your own home via a digitally connected machine)?

The likelihood is a retailer already exists that is not satisfied with just improving continuously what has gone before. History is littered with examples of companies redefining how consumers needs are met.

In some ways it is not significant defects in Category Management that are delivering a just ok retail experience. Fundamentally Category Management is built to support and reflect the retailers corporate objectives. Look at some of these and you will understand why this is creating a grey retail landscape.

Mission statements are littered with "best price" "lowest price" "creating value" comments. Once they delivered an edge over a more fragmented, costly and inconsistent market place serviced by small chains and independent operators.

That world does not exist anymore in most developed markets.

The move from "I go shopping because I have to" towards "I go shopping because I want to have fun, be excited, be challenged, feel successful, feel sexy, be loved and accepted" is coming and Retail Shopper Management is a step in the right direction.

But it doesn't stop there.

If retailers are to share some of the responsibility for the defective nature of Category Management, which puts it at risk, then manufacturers must too.

For most of my career I have worked with some of the largest international manufacturers around the world. I have seen their attempts to use Category Management to advance their brands and profits.

So if Category Management is alive and well in packaged consumer goods could I ask all the retailers reading this to answer a simple question. How many times has a manufacturer walked through your door and told you to delist some of their products because a competitor meets consumers needs in a better way? I thought not.

So if you start from a position of bias, towards "doing the numbers" at the expense of the truth, what credibility do you expect to have with a Category Manager? An attitude of "I will share the information that allows me to sell more of my product" will not build a collaborative environment where real value can be added.

It also does not help the situation when manufacturers focus on product push rather than pull. Distribution, range, stock. Get the product in front of shoppers at all costs. Who cares if it is a me too product which cannibalises existing sales and adds zero to a retailers bottom line? "This market is an opportunity for us and we need to be part of it. Get it listed". Sound familiar?

When Category Management goes off the rails as a concept it often revolves around a lack of the commercial reality that exists between retailers and manufacturers.

Consultancies that bleat on about both sides working in partnership and seeing "the big picture" are deluded at best. When times are tough and commercial targets have to be met I don't know a major business out there that wouldn't cheerfully run a lawn mower over the other party if it meant making the necessary profit to satisfy shareholders.

What retail CEO would give a manufacturer an easy time if it meant jeopardising his career, family security and long term retirement plans?

What manufacturing CEO would halve his range because it was the "right thing to do for retailers" based on a Category Management exercise and risk the investor back lash when dividends drop?

Believing that higher, long term, strategic Category Management principles will stand that acid test is no more than marketing masturbation.

Does this mean that it can't happen? No. I believe that many of the excellent principles in Category Management have a significant part to play in delivering some magic and affect how we will shop in the future and what we get out of it.

To get there, though, we need to have a realistic view of where we are, what's causing the problems and how each side needs to change to deliver a shopper experience which not only satisfies core needs but also enriches their lives through experiential input.

3 RETAILER VS MANUFACTURER
OR
"HOW DID TAKING A WARM SHOWER WITH MY PARTNER TURN INTO A SCENE FROM PSYCHO?"

In 2009 Tesco in the UK hit the headlines when it allegedly summoned suppliers to its offices and demanded additional support payments. Numbers up to £750,000 ($1,200,000 at today's exchange rate) were reported to have been discussed.

Manufacturers complained to the press, often anonymously, that they were being treated unfairly. Boo hoo!

Are they serious? If the MD of any supplier swapped places with a retail MD wouldn't he or she try to buy at a lower price? I made that move from manufacturer to retailer and guess what, I brought the same commitment to increasing profits as a buyer as I did as an account manager and so would they. Suppliers have the option to just say no. If they can't say no then it may be because their products are too substitutional and not competitive anymore or they do not add value in other ways.

If they can't take the heat get out of the super value, in store restaurants kitchen. Look I know this is harsh but to deal with this type of behaviour you need different skills. Relying on a historical partnership won't cut it.

I would be interested to hear the conversation. Do you think it went like this. "But we have been working together driving your category. How can you ask for more support?"

The question is this. At any time in terms negotiations does Category Management play a part or is it just about moving cash from the manufacturer to the retailer? Category Management is quickly abandoned in the face of commercial pressures.

This scene is replicated around the globe continuously. I have worked in countries from the USA to Japan. From Russia to South Africa and many places in between.

At no time did I see a change in behaviour. Sometimes there are cultural differences in the sales teams but buyers are buyers. They ask, they don't offer.

For Category Management to work it has to encourage both parties to share information and join in an agreed partnership.

At times in supplier/manufacturer relationships it is advantageous for the two businesses to work towards the same goals but once that period is at an end it becomes an unbalanced power play.

Suppliers have no more consumer insight to trade and retailers have a choice of supply that they can leverage.

This is the key difference between Category Management in retailers vs manufacturers. If a retailer needs to fill a market opportunity by satisfying newly exposed customer trends, needs or behaviour, they can go to any supplier or develop own brand solutions. Manufacturers have only their existing range to look to. Maybe R&D can come up with a solution in six months "if marketing gets its act together for once" but it will always struggle to react as fast.

Even when you have intrinsic links between both organisations such as Vendor Inventory Management (where a manufacturer takes responsibility for maximising on shelf availability) it may seem that true collaboration, to reduce costs and increase profits, is happening but the truth is it can be purely a superficial negotiation tactic.

Here is a simple example. Category Captains. They may be described as Category Partners, Advisors, Validators or a dozen different names but in truth it is often a way of seducing a key supplier into providing additional financial support for little or no return.

"We are seeking a Category Captain for this department and have to choose between you and your nearest competitor. It will cost you $100,000. If you agree to it we will choose you because we believe you are hungry to develop the business".

In return they get the chance to wear the invisible Category Captain hat and badge. They also get to do all the work a retailer should do. Planograms, merchandising layouts, product listing forms plus supplying all of their consumer data for free.

Now I know what every Category Captain will be saying. "We get to specify our layout". Do they really think any retailer would agree a planogram that did not meet their objectives?

In some instances they do make short term gains for both companies. But are the massive additional profits they generate for the total store and chain reflected in their annual terms negotiation?

If they truly want to know if they are Category Captains perhaps they need to ask themselves some simple questions.

When they share consumer data for free do they have to pay for data from the retailer either in total or as part of their annual fee?
Do retailers charge them to be a "Category Partner"?
Does it feel like a collaborative partnership at CEO level while the Account Manager is being roasted on a spit everyday by the buyers?
Do they earn lower cash profits and take on higher cash costs from initiatives?

If they answered yes to any of these then they may want to resign from the Category Captains job before the ship goes down. My son bought a toy captains hat and a sheriffs badge to play with when he was five. They cost $5. I think he was ripped off by the retailer. How much did a Category Captains cost? Maybe my sons was a good deal after all. If there are any reading this and they are interested in his hat and badge I am certain he will resell them to them for half the cost they are paying for theirs, because he likes them. Honestly. Better than their competitors. Trust him.

Realisation of this truth could put Category Management in serious danger.

Let's be serious for a moment though. It's not always like this. In some exceptional circumstances it is closer to a collaborative partnership but this happens when both sides keep a clear vision of what can be achieved in the longer term. Even in this environment it would be foolish to believe that the other party will keep themselves honest.

Later in this book we get to understand how to bring reality to a theoretically perfect world which is actually anything but and this could possibly have saved Category Managements life.

We show how to understand the truth behind the misconceptions and help both sides manage their own financial success in a future where Retail Shopper Management will change the rules of engagement completely.

Before we skip off down this yellow brick road to retailing Oz we need to understand the issues from a retail perspective.

It's all very well for manufacturers to believe that it's just the evil retailers taking their consumer insight and then tearing up the partnership when they need the margin but, in truth, there is much for manufacturers to consider about their behaviour.

It starts as simply as the account manager arriving for a meeting with a buyer.

As soon as he or she enters the room the first thing they do is start asking about the buyers family, interests, hobbies, life.

Why?

Simply they want to generate a relationship which helps them get what they want.

It's no different to a guy listening intently to a girls life story when his only intension is getting her into bed and then never returning her calls.

Can you imagine how many times a buyer gets asked these same questions every week? Does the Account Manager really care if a buyers child is getting on well at his new school or if the weather on holiday was good? Buyers are not stupid. They know it is completely superficial with most salespeople.

This may seem a simplistic view but it is the foundation of falsehoods that a house of trust and openness will be built on. It's no surprise then that it crashes down periodically if this is where it starts.

Professional buyers know that manufacturers prize the quality of relationship. If you were a buyer and understood it was really important for a supplier to have a good relationship with you what would you do? Would you use that against them if the business demanded it?

If it is important to build a collaborative relationship why do retailers change their teams regularly? They do it to add challenge to the business relationship not to strengthen it.

Some people may think that the partnership is ok at higher levels in their business and that problems are caused by the sales people, not reflecting Senior Management initiatives and collaborative behaviours. If so try this on for size.

Ask your sales team to provide anonymous feedback on senior managers.

One question.

"Has a senior manager ever circumvented your authority by giving something away in a negotiation that you never would and he or she did not get a tangible cash return?"

I have asked this of commercial teams for years because retail buyers are trained to target high level executives with big budgets, large egos and little detailed information on how the account generates profit. It is always the same answer.

A typical response is "The retailers CEO challenged our GM to show he was serious and wanted us to prove we wanted to be part of their business. The next minute he gave away $50,000 additional support for very little just to buy a relationship".

The last time I heard of money changing hands to buy a relationship it was called prostitution.

Giving something away without getting a relative value return actively encourages retailers to treat manufacturers this way so why do manufacturers think they deserve a partnership?

In fact it goes deeper than this. If a manufacturer wouldn't damage their own business by telling the truth about a Category Management exercise and retailers know this, why should a buyer ever believe one word that comes out of their mouths. Welcome to the game. Now the fun starts.

It's easy to have noble values about delivering positive retail benefits, like adding additional shoppers to a retailers base, when it benefits you. It's not so easy to be noble when it means reducing your range.

This relationship is not an easy one to manage.

So where are we so far? We have uncovered a lot of clues in our search for the why and who of this tragic case.

The retail landscape is too cloned.
Differentiation is not a byproduct of Category Management.
At best it is delivering a credible point of purchase that satisfies a geographically distressed need to buy.
At worst it ignores the wider picture by focusing on the shopper within category rather than the shopper within the world he or she exists.
The belief that low prices and quality product will win lifetime

loyal customers is outdated.

Category Management does not drive an aspirational objective for retailers, and for manufacturers it is either something they get beaten with tactically or they use tactically to extend their range.

As an industry we are largely delusional when it comes to our interpretation of excitement for shoppers and consumers.

The trusting relationship required to make Category Management work is periodically destabilised, intentionally or unintentionally, by business pressures.

The focus remains on superficial needs of consumers, not the deep seated emotional ones that offer a real point of difference for shoppers.

All of this is may be valid but is not enough to justify murder. What else are we missing?

Let's talk about how retailers and manufacturers could benefit from closer relationships in the real world.

First we need to understand how to engage with retailers. Many books have been written on the subject but I am a simple person so let's not wrap ourselves up in consultancy jibber jabber.

Some people say it's all about understanding a retailers needs. Try asking that question of your customer and you will get slapped around the face with comments like more percentage margin, better support, bigger promotions, longer payment terms. None of which are close to their real needs. They have actually just told you their personal KPIs. It's not the same.

Retailers actually want a manufacturer to help them sell more, to more shoppers, more often. That's pretty simple isn't it? Yes they do want it to happen from an optimised stock base, efficient logistics operation, with higher cash margins and more favourable payment terms but more, to more people more often is the deal.

More = larger shopping baskets and or higher ticket prices that typically carry better cash margins.

More shoppers = new customers from the available opportunity pool capable of shopping at that location or in that chain

More often = increasing not only the frequency of visit to store by shoppers but increasing in store conversion which drives higher frequency of purchase.

Later in the book we can expand this simple view to offer far greater insight into opportunities but for now lets stick with it.

Increasing these three mechanics can be achieved in a variety of ways; deals designed to up-trade, package promotions, cross category bundling of products targeted at events eg BBQ season, coupon redemption schemes, exclusive products, the list goes on and on.

In a non expandable market place part of the game is about polarising shoppers to a particular retailer, adding value to them and gaining them additional share of pocket.

By non expandable I mean limited by natural consumption. An example of this is toilet tissue. When you walk into a supermarket and purchase a buy one get one free deal on multipacks you don't instantly run home to use the toilet twice as much. You have simply increased your in home stock level.

In these non expandable markets manufacturers win by cannibalising competitors sales and attracting them to their own brands.

Both companies can make additional profits in non saturated markets by helping each other achieve these objectives. A retailer may favour one manufacturer in a category if, in return, that manufacturer provides a competitive edge over the retailers direct competition.

The retailer gets a new customer and the manufacturer potentially gets a new consumer. If both can be retained over a long period the value is high on both sides.

These relationships are often very one dimensional and last a relatively short period of time though. Competition catches up and then everything re balances. There is a difference between a competitive edge and a sustainable competitive edge.

In saturated markets it becomes more difficult. Does the Heinz company care whether it's consumers buy Tomato Ketchup in

Walmart or Kmart? Not really unless terms and, therefore, net profits differ slightly. Does Apple mind which phone provider supplies an iPhone?

There is less for retailers to offer in return for stocking these products. On the contrary, high brand loyal products like these make it difficult for retailers to negotiate better prices. It doesn't stop them trying though.

In expandable markets things get a lot more interesting and the opportunity for driving higher profits increases significantly.

How can manufacturers help drive a markets expansion? Again let's keep the answer at the same simplistic level. It's all about encouraging more consumption, by more consumers, more often.

Take fast food restaurants as an example. They sell more to more people more often by encouraging consumers to eat more (meal deals), eaten by more people (salads
penetrating the health conscious consumer group) eaten more often (an offer for breakfast delivering an additional consumption event).

Sales of product into retailers is largely irrelevant in developing solid, profitable businesses. In the long term it's sales out to shoppers that is key. Consumer pull beats supplier push everyday of the week.

Yes, sometimes it is required to drive distribution but neglecting generating shopper pull by failing to develop innovative, smart activities is low level thinking.

The objective is to make a store THE POINT OF PURCHASE on every visit not just a CREDIBLE POINT OF PURCHASE.

Failure to effectively promote your range opens the door for your competitors. They get the chance to own your consumer base in that store. If you continue down this road and they then take the initiative it will only be a matter of time before they become dominant.

In some categories high brand loyalty and daily staple products like dairy, diapers and baby formula mean that product naturally disappears off the shelves.

It doesn't mean that a manufacturer is doing a great job and playing their part in making a retailer THE point of purchase in the mind of a shopper.

Many retailers and manufacturers talk about "destination". Destination stores, destination products, destination categories and destination brands.

At this point I just want to focus for a minute on destination point of purchase.

It's not just A place I buy a product, category or service it is THE ONLY place I will buy a product, category or service (unless I am geographically displaced).

Being geographically displaced turns it into a distressed sale.

In the small lakeside town where I live there is a great cafe culture. Sunday mornings you will always find a crowd of people taking coffee outside restaurants from early morning even in the middle of winter.

Occasionally I treat myself to the four "C's". A cigar, a coffee, a cognac and a croissant while I sit and enjoy the view. It's a well balanced diet.

I have two options to buy my cigar for this event. First and cheapest is the newsagent on the right hand side of my favourite restaurant. Product is good quality, well kept and great value.

The other option is the cigar shop to the left of the restaurant. I buy my over priced product there.

This is not just a tobacconist it's an emotional smorgasbord. They have huge leather seating if you are enjoying a product or just socialising. The seats are so grand you would expect to look up and not be surprised to see Churchill and Roosevelt sitting opposite you discussing global strategy. A walk in humidor full of exotic and rare product fills a third of the shop. Stunning displays of paraphernalia are everywhere. The owner is fantastic and tells me all about the different brands which are similar and why others are so different. He knows I will buy the same one I always do but he engages me emotionally with the way he talks.

As I leave with my purchase I nod to the other customers in that way that says "we are all part of this great fantasy club".

My challenge to retailers is this. What shopper needs are you satisfying so well that you own them for this sale and the next, forever? And it's not price, quality, service, convenience. Look around you. Your nearest two competitors are doing the same.

It's about consumers and shoppers. Their emotions. Their view of themselves. How you add to their lives in more fundamental ways. Like Starbucks providing love and belonging.

You can keep trying to use Category Management to deliver a competitive edge but make certain you have a good exit package negotiated when market shares and profits slide.

Price, product, and promotion can be too easily copied and service/quality are givens.

Category Management has a key role to play in developing solutions to maximising profits but ignoring shoppers wider desires, fantasies and psychological drivers will prevent you becoming THE destination for their next purchase.

You will just be a me too. Interchangeable. Replaceable.

For manufacturers the challenge is what part are you playing in your partnership with retailers to help them achieve a real point of difference that matters to shoppers? Do you honestly care? In a world, where many manufacturers now get direct access to consumers through internet sales, is it important to drive consumers to a specific retailer? Well yes, if that also offers you long term profit opportunities.

In an environment of natural distrust finding a solution will not be easy. It becomes especially difficult if we ignore the truth that there is little reason for large retailers and manufacturers to trust each other in the long term.

But I like a challenge.

Let's see if we can find an answer before the end of the book and if we could have saved Category Managements life?

4 CATEGORY MANAGEMENT IN RETAIL
OR
"WHY IS THERE A CLOWN IN MY SHOPPING CART?"

20 years ago retail looked completely different. Not just externally to its customers but internally due to the way it was structured.

Pre the introduction of Category Managers into most retail chains, buyers took on a different role completely.

A buyer would not only negotiate pricing and select product, they would also get involved in specifying promotional merchandising layouts, promotion development, product development and design plus a multitude of marketing activities.

They were retail experts who occupied a generalist role. By using their knowledge of the detail behind their specialist product groups to engage with shoppers they increased sales and profits.

Over the subsequent years a Henry Ford approach to retailing has completely changed the way businesses are managed. Each function has been split away from the generalist role and developed into much narrower, specialised position.

Category Managers create strategy and support this with appropriate ranges. Buyers get the right price. Product Managers secure promotion and drive sale rates and mix. Merchandisers develop POS and display. The list goes on.

Each role is focused, in many retailers, at viewing the Category as one single business unit.

Over the last few years it has become more apparent that viewing the shopper as only a customer of the category limits opportunities across the rest of the store.

In destination categories which deliver daily staples, such as bakery and dairy in grocers, the importance of these products driving footfall into store has never been underestimated.

Now it has become more apparent that other unique products and brands deliver consumers to retail stores and removal of one of these can make a shopper switch a shopping event to another retailer.

Conversely, focused micro marketing (selecting range based on local anomalies in buyer preference and behaviour) can add new customers to a store.

A good example of this occurs close to where I live in Switzerland. Geneva is balanced on the boarder with France and attracts a massive expat community made up by many Americans and British citizens.

Trying to find some classic brands from your home country, ones that are difficult to replace by alternatives, turns into a full time event when it comes to managing the weekly shopping trips.

In response to this Carrefour has innovated a specific international aisle which is conveniently segmented by nationality.

The store is 5 minutes over the boarder into France and stocks products from Britain, America, Spain etc. Brands such as Colman's mustard, Heinz Baked Beans, Hershey's chocolate are displayed in prime position.

They are targeted at each expat community with the view to making this store destination for a weekly shopping event. Guess what, it works. When new people arrive word of mouth lets them know where they can get their fix of Marmite, peanut butter or maple syrup. And when they are there they obviously complete their primary shopping purchases.

This type of initiative is supported by the idea that there needs to be a "Shopper Manager" role introduced to compliment this approach.

Shopper Managers can look wider at different needs that make cross category promotions more successful.

I am not just talking about traditional event promotions like BBQ season displays but more importantly Baby and Toddler sections attracting new families to select a location for its change in life stage.

Support from manufacturers in supplying insight for their specialist area of expertise is useful but because it is often "filtered" to support increased ranging for that specific company it can be limited.

It can also be very tunnel vision, focused at areas of importance and opportunity to that specific manufacturer. We saw earlier where a Category Manager could make a decision that will benefit them but reduce profits across the store. Manufacturers insight data can also be weighted in favour of a category. This will again give a distorted outcome.

If retailers really want to see shoppers and consumers in crystal clear clarity, taking control of data is key.

But not just data about purchase behaviour, sale rates, market trends, consumer insights, market share (macro and micro) etc.

You have to look deeper into shoppers and consumers social and psychological needs to really have a chance at owning them as a long term customer.

Let's look at the Disney company for some examples of what I am getting at.

When Walt Disney had a vision for Disneyland, where adults and children could go to be entertained together, he set in motion one of the most amazing money generating machines imagined.

During presentations on retail strategies I often ask the question "what are Disneyland and Disney World?"

The answer is always the same. Theme Parks.

Is that really what they think they are?

If you have ever walked onto Main Street USA through those giant gates how old did you feel? The first time I walked into the Orlando park I was 28. I was with 7 friends about the same age. It was truly magical to watch. In seconds we were all 5 years old again and we stayed like it all week.

At the end of the holiday we all had to buy additional suitcases to bring back the vast array of merchandise we bought.

It took a month to get rid of the weight I put on eating and drinking park food.

It then occurred to me what Disney Parks are. They are shops. Giant shops. Surrounded by a sea of restaurants. The way we are convinced to go shopping there is by making us laugh, scream and feel.

Experiential retailing at its best.

Even today Disney continues to evolve and add value in non tangible ways. The latest TV adverts shows a father and his teenage daughter. It suggests that she doesn't normally want to be on holiday with her parents at that age but the way to have her still want to spend time with you is to take her to Disney World.

Come to my store and you get your little girl back for a week. I would suggest that isn't the typical benefit you would expect a retailer to satisfy. It's a little different from EDLP (Every Day Low Prices) but far more powerful.

Try to bring that approach out with a category scorecard!

I am not suggesting getting rid of EDLP in favour of a water slide though Home-care into Wines and Spirits.

What I am saying is that somewhere between the two are some great benefits you can offer beyond the norm.

Later I come back to this and try to offer some ideas on how to re invent your customer offer.

For now, let's move on.

In a world which is competing on the internet, experiential retailing is a key way to differentiate the act of acquiring compared to the experience of acquiring. I believe it can go further to deliver emotions while acquiring.

The current path we are on is norming the results. New software aimed at delivering faster, more optimum assortments may ultimately produce outputs that reduce differentiation.

There is a joke about two tourists driving through the countryside. They get lost and stop to ask a local man, standing beside the road, the way to the nearest town.

"You want to get to town? He says. "Ummm. You don't want to start from here".

Perhaps the journey to meeting shopper and consumer needs does not start from where we are now either. Maybe we need to start somewhere else.

But first we need to look at the realities of Category Management in manufacturing and what realistically we can expect from it. Did manufacturing have a part to play in its demise?

5 CATEGORY MANAGEMENT IN MANUFACTURERS
OR
"WHICH SHELL IS THE PEA UNDER?"

In 2009 I joined Japan Tobacco International (JTI) and had the chance to work with Chris Powell who was strategic director for global key account management in their World Wide Duty Free division at that time.

Chris is a visionary character who has very clear views on manufacturers and the benefits they can bring to retailers.

He pioneered changes in the Travel Retail market, particularly in airports, that are still having repercussions today.

Over his time working with tobacco he realised the win a retailer could get from his high loyalty, branded products, was not just the profit they received from a sale in the category. It was mostly the additional purchases his consumers made in the other categories.

His brands brought new customers to travel retail stores.

Rather than just leverage this position of power, purely to benefit his own business, he raised his thinking to store level.

When talking to retailers he was clear that it was important not to exclude key brands (even competitors) because de-listing them would be the same as "de-listing a shopper" as Chris put it.

If you have ever seen Chris present you will have been under no illusions that his ultimate goal was driving the success of the other categories by leveraging his destination category, destination products and destination brands.

I have heard the words spoken by many other manufacturers in other industries but Chris is the only person I have seen back it up with the real, consistent action that delivers results.

In this sector JTI is famous for its approach which puts retail success at the heart of its strategy and consumers at the heart of retail.

Although Chris has moved on, the team continues to work with retailers to add value by understanding as much about shopper and consumer behaviour as possible.

It's a clear, publicised strategy that the whole division, from GM down, is signed up to achieving. It's business has been structured to realise this objective and all members of the sales, marketing and data intelligence teams have been personally developed to be able to add value to the process. It even includes sales support functions such as Finance and HR in that same development path.

The commitment to making it happen is business wide and many of the star members of the team are now driving the benefits deeper into the JTI customer base, helping develop some real partnerships. In fact some of the junior team are a powerhouse for change.

In this situation a manufacturer walks the talk and, not only helps manage the categories success, but also looks at the shopper in the wider context of the store. It is the reason they have begun winning industry awards.

This provides them with a mid term competitive edge that could become a sustainable one if the momentum continues.

During my time with JTI I had the privilege to also work with Andy Boynton, Dean at the Carroll School of Management at Boston College and co author of "The Idea Hunter".

Andy has brought clarity, strategic direction and, more importantly, profits to the largest companies on the planet. His ability to cut through the BS and focus a team is legendary.

He is all about energy and leadership. Spend a day with him and you will feed off it for a year.

One of the key things I learned working with Andy was that, in some special businesses, competitive edge can be delivered by the way the people in it interact. Culture is very difficult to copy, clone or imitate. A business filled with people who have a shared vision of the future, a mentality of treating the impossible as an everyday task and a drive to deliver something special is impossible to replicate easily. This can be a sustainable competitive edge. In fact one of the few ways it can be destroyed is if there is a lack of leadership which fails to empower individuals to be all they can be. I have seen it happen and the best way I can describe it is Corporate Mediocrity.

Corporate mediocrity is a disease and like most diseases it has carriers.

Low level, high ranked people who carry the genes and transfer them to their virtual offspring.

Driven by fear of risk and a culture of ok is ok, they infect the weak and weaken the strong. Often great words of inspiration are spoken but, in reality, there is no substance to any of them.

Culture is a double edged sword.

If you get it right though, it leaves your competitors searching for traditional ways to compete which, ultimately, fail to deliver the same impact.

Getting back to tobacco though we have to understand it is a very unusual product for many reasons. Extreme brand loyalty for starters.

In the Travel Retail environment a tobacco manufacturer has more chance to positively impact store and chain profits. It is the only real daily staple purchased by an easily targetable, significant consumer group which is sold in most of these stores. Therefore it is critical to maximise its power to deliver shoppers to store where they can be sold other category's such as confectionary and liqueur.

However in a classic FMCG environment a manufacturer of bottled water will not have the same opportunities. It may still have a part to play but, ultimately, substitutional products like many bottled waters will live and die based on selling/negotiation skills, stock turn, logistics benefits and low manufacturing costs.

Take, for instance, the initiative Darren Blackhurst, the then Chief Merchandising Officer at Asda Walmart, brought in in 2007. He realised there were many branded products that were completely substitutional. In fact, in the eyes of most of his shoppers, they were not real brands at all.

Yes their names were well known but, in actual fact, they had fallen into the same situation many retailers are in now.

All their brand did was make them a "credible choice" for shoppers, not THE choice.

Every attribute that originally made them successful historically had been duplicated. Quality, pack size, variety, price. Nothing now differentiated them and so they could be eliminated from the range with no loss of shoppers.

They completely failed to secure a unique place in the emotions of their consumers. They also failed to replace their traditional consumer benefits with new ones.

Over time their old ones became commonplace and they had mistaken brand recall and market share for brand loyalty.

For some manufacturers, a Category Management analysis and score carding exercise will be a terrifying prospect as it exposes their vulnerability to being replaced. It does, however, highlight ares where they can be less substitutional. Stock management and logistics for instance.

For many years PepsiCo have utilised its extraordinary ability to get its Frito-Lay snack products to store in the most competitive way for its own and retailers benefits.

Across different markets it brings a mixture of direct to store, distributor delivery and a multitude of other combinations to give it leadership in fulfilling on shelf availability demands without incurring uncompetitive costs. Even in situations where daily replenishment to store is required.

This ability to reach retail points of purchase, in a way that adds value to retail and makes it difficult for them to be substituted as a business, has helped give them a sustainable competitive edge for decades.

It has little to do with their latest flavour of Doritos which, I am certain, will be impossible to stop eating until the packet is empty.

I may know the weight and frequency of consumption of its new products will produce consumer pull but there are more important considerations that make them special.

As a retailer, Frito-Lay is just as important to me because they have very low on-shelf out of stocks, low days cover (the amount of stock in the chain which covers the daily sale rate) and they increase my GMROII (Gross Margin Return On Inventory Investment).

Living within the bounds of Category Management is comfortable for many manufacturers. They use it to successfully develop products that meet emerging trends for instance.

Let's see how it works in manufacturing with a simple test. I would like to pose the following scenario for all manufacturers reading this and ask you to choose one of the
options at the end. I would like you do it honestly based on the culture and business pressures you live under.

The business case:

You are now the Commercial Director of a mid sized North

American pharmaceutical company specialising in baby and toddler products. Your number one product is the market leading baby formula. You have a 23% market share. The number 2 brand, from your biggest competitor, sits at 21%.

Your brand has been available for over 30 years and is known by every household in the USA.

Over the last 4 years you have seen an increase in organic baby foods designed to help a baby's early development. In parallel with this your company has developed a range of natural minerals and vitamins which have just completed clinical trials.

The amazing news is that they have been proven, by independent verification, to increase toddlers attention span by 50%, their problem solving ability by 20% and overall IQ by 15%. The new product "Organic Baby Genius Booster" is revolutionary and a cast iron success based on all market predictions!

To support it's sell in you have also instigated a Category Management exercise including a new consumer insight survey.

You have just had the result delivered and it's catastrophic news. Organic Baby Genius Booster is right on track for the success you anticipated but the bad news is about your traditional baby formula product which accounts for 20% of your annual sales.

A lack of investment in new production facilities means that it is now becoming uncompetitive in the market place. A new factory is being built but will not come on line for 18 months. This means you have to increase prices. Not good considering the product maintains its sale rate by periodic promotion which retailers expect you to fund.

Even worse than this, consumer feedback shows that it is completely substitutional and new parents are happy to choose either leading brand. Your competitor has invested in new facilities and by your guess they can offer a higher cash margin to retailers and still be more profitable than you.

You know when the price increase goes through it will probably suppress retail margins even more because your competitors recommended retail price will prevent the retailer increasing yours. You also know you have no choice. It has been made quite clear to you the financing of the business, at this moment in time, requires a prices rise.

You have to make a presentation to the retailer. There are only 3 options based on the financials you have looked at. Which choice would you make?

Option 1:
Tell the truth.
Explain that part of your range is uncompetitive and substitutional. Common sense says the retailer should de-list the old product until the new factory comes on line and it is re- launched to make the brand more modern and unique. In the meantime you have a great opportunity with Baby Genius Booster which could drive a whole new aisle focused at baby organic and health products.

Option 2:
Tell a lie.
Only present the good news about the new product launch and bury the negative feedback on the old products substitutional situation. In fact, when the price increase goes through and margins are depressed you highlight its number one market share and explain it is impossible to de-list the market leader. The retailer will just have to live with lower margins.

Option 3:
Trade Baby Genius Booster.
Explain the facts that you are about to launch the "must have" product for baby and toddlers which will generate millions of dollars and you are seeking launch partners. If the retailer agrees to develop a completely new "Organic and Health" aisle and support your products better by co-funding promotions on the old baby formula you will sign them up for the launch.

Which one would you choose?

More importantly which do you think a retailer believes you would choose?

This is inherently the issue with this situation. Even if you tell the truth there is often a natural distrust between the two organisations because manufacturers do not, on a regular basis, deliver bad news about their products.

Most manufacturers defend them and try to maintain the existing range while pushing for product and distribution extensions.

Behaviour such as this, in this environment, makes it is very difficult to be taken seriously as a real business partner.

Conversely, I will hazard a guess, there will be very few manufacturers who haven't been on the wrong end of tactical behaviour from retailers. Even those who strive to develop long term partnerships will be driven to lower prices, increase support and take on more of the retailers overheads.

As you can see from the chart below the move of costs from retailer to manufacturer over the last 20 years is impressive and I only mention a few ways they have managed it.

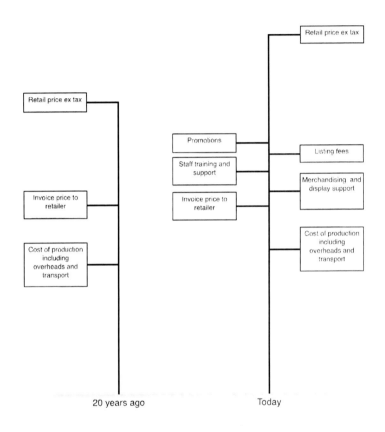

20 years ago   Today

When Category Management works for both sides it adds value to the total profit pie. The reality is that many consultancies (and I am certain they will spend the rest of their marketing budget to rubbish this view, well, wouldn't you?) want to tell you that manufacturers should let retailers do the right thing for the category and provide support to deliver profits.

Seriously. What half arsed, delusional world do they live in. So manufacturers should drop their commercial trousers and hand over the keys to the treasury?

Be real. Category Management is over ruled by share holders, dividends, bonuses, school fees and pensions. It is also secondary to mortgages, alimony fees and car payments.

If, in their beautiful, well organised, perfectly structured view of retailing Nirvana they think the behaviour of most retailers is going to encourage manufactures to give up the Crown Jewels without a certain apprehension they should come see me and I can do them a great deal on some real estate in the Everglades.

And I promise to call you in the morning. Because I love you. Really. You are very special to me. Really. Special. Really!

I used the expression "half arsed"? Not many business books use that type of terminology. Actually, I am not going to apologise. If they think that's bad wait until they see their clients lose 5% market share and profits erode within a few weeks. They may want to thank me then as I may spur them into action before the whirlwind comes in. And this does happen. Look back on the trading figures for the last 10 years peak periods in FMCG and you will see that even some of the biggest and most successful retailers have lost share, profit and stock value due to their substitutional vulnerability.

Let me be very clear here. It is not in the long term interests of retailers to maintain a collaborative relationship with a manufacturer 100% of the time. Why? Because manufacturers become complacent and standards drop while margins (manufacturer margins) increase.

On the other side of the coin, retailers will ask manufacturers for the world on a stick and be upset that it it's not wrapped with a bow when it arrives. Why? Because they are trained to do it. It's their job.

It's what they do every day, all day.

Traditional Category Management puts itself in the firing line because it lacks a link to reality. If moving towards Retail Shopper Management is a realistic solution, which will increase ambition levels for retailers and manufacturers in line with consumers increasing need for stimulation, then we have to recognise there is a missing piece of the puzzle that has to be integrated into the process.

That piece of the puzzle deals with human behaviour. It recognises it is an imperfect world and that it is never going to change. Welcome to the real world, now let's deal with it.

6 WELCOME TO THE GAME
OR
"WHO STOLE MY PIE?"

The morning was cool. Light mist hung in the valley between the trees and stuck to the leaves. This was typical of a morning in early March 148,657 years BC.

Last year there was still some snow on the ground at this time but this year it had melted early which had made his trip to the river to catch fish much easier.

He was good at catching fish. He was the best in the tribe. He had worked out long ago where the fish rested in the river and knew exactly where to spear them. He could catch ten fish in the time it took most of the others to catch one.

There were always too many fish for him to eat himself and he often gave one to the old man that used to take him hunting when he was a boy. It was one of the few things the elder could still eat because most of teeth had now disappeared.

It had been a good morning at the river. Seven fish were slung on his spear and he carried it across his shoulder. As the fisherman walked into the clearing with his catch he saw the woman he called Scar. When she was younger she had fallen into a gully and sliced a deep wound into her upper arm. At the time he thought she might get the fever and die like his brother had, but she recovered. The cut had left a white, vertical scar as long as his middle finger.

She had some big leaves in her arms all wrapped up to make a basket. Laying inside were large piles of berries. They were dark and richly red stained the leaves. She must have taken hours to pick the enormous quantity she had. They would come in handy to feed her 6 children.

As he arrived at his hut she walked past, eyeing the fish. He eyed the berries. They smiled at each other.

He waved for her to stop and he pointed at the berries and then the fish. She looked from one to the other slowly. After a few minutes she realised he was suggesting an exchange. She smiled and nodded. She pointed to the fish and held up two fingers and then pointed to the berries and scooped out a big handful.

Two fish for one handful of berries did not make sense to him. Something in his head said that big smile on her face showed the deal was making her very happy. Too happy. He pointed at two fish and then the berries and waved four fingers in front of her. Her smile disappeared.

Now she had a frown. She had walked for miles to find the berries. They were hard to pick and she had been scratched many times. Two fish for four handfuls did not leave her with enough for her children. She held up three fingers.

They both nodded and the exchange was completed. He looked forward to eating the berries later after the fish. He still had two fish for himself, a fish for the old man and the air was still so cold that the other two should be ok to eat tomorrow. He started to build a fire.

Scar walked back to her hut and as she arrived the hunter, that she occasionally saw on her foraging days, walked through the village and stopped as he came level with her.

He pointed at the fish and the held up a rabbit he had caught. She hated rabbit and shook her head but then pointed down the village to the fisherman's hut.

He waved and headed towards the man now sitting in front of a small fire he was trying, rather unsuccessfully, to light.

The hunter looked at the fish, he loved fish. The rabbits were easy to catch but, after a while, he got bored with the taste. He pointed to two fish and held up the rabbit.

The fisherman shook his head and held up one finger. The hunter shook his head. This trade was not going to work. Then the hunter looked down at the miserable attempt at the fire and had an idea. He used his rudimentary words to explain that, in return for the two fish, he could light and build the fire for the fisherman plus he could give him a rabbit.

Now this made sense to the fisherman and they agreed on the trade.

This was the 7th of March 148,657 BC. The day that retailing, trading, negotiation, employment, business management, capitalism, stock management, gross margin, category management and profit was invented. It's been downhill from there ever since.

Over the next few months other tribes discovered the fisherman's hut was the place you could trade for fresh foods, fruit and sometimes other items. The fisherman soon discovered what goods the others wanted and what they didn't. He knew that some people only came to him once during the moons cycle while others came everyday. He made certain he found out what they wanted and why they came at certain times. This meant he did not waste food and could get the best return.

After six moons he was so good at it he even had to teach two of Scars children how to fish because he didn't have time anymore. He spent all his time at the hut trading.

He had now invented The Game as I politely describe it to manufacturers I work with.

The Game is the beautiful ballet that is danced between retailers

47

and manufacturers over the creation of profit for the two companies and the decision where that profit ends up.

At times it feels like a conversation between lovers and within days the same people can be involved in behaviour more appropriate between America and the Soviet Union at the height of the Cold War.

We are obviously getting into the wonderful, exciting and beautiful world of negotiation.

It's fantastic to observe from outside but can be emotionally draining for those involved.

Many people in manufacturing, especially Account Managers, Sales Directors and even CEOs believe it is a skill they have in their arsenal. The difference for retailers is that they know they have it in theirs. Retail negotiators are the lions in the jungle. If you want to go hunting them you better go well armed.

They are well trained. Mostly by professionals, but always by sales people. Every time they get something for free from an Account Manager it encourages them to ask for more. Every time a Commercial Director gives a better deal to build a "relationship" it teaches them to bypass the Account Manager who's credibility is now zero.

One word of advice for manufacturers who have a sales team and deal with FMCG retailers. Get them trained and once they are trained get them trained again and again. Start with the CEO and cascade it down through the business. Make it a real part of their lives and a valued skill. The Return On Investment (ROI) will be enormous.

I have had the chance to work with a team of people in the UK who, based on the experience I have had around the world, are simply the best in FMCG commercial skills development.

Sentinel Management Consultants, headed up by their CEO Dave Sables, are real business professionals.

The team is a mixture of ex buyers and senior sales directors. They set themselves as the antidote to the tactical nature of retailers. They have helped manufacturers around the world build more successful and competitive businesses for over 15 years.

They do this by integrating, highly advanced selling and negotiation skills, into the commercial disciplines manufacturers require to function in today's FMCG market place.

Marketing, distributor management, consumer insights, shopper analysis and logistics are all seamlessly woven into Sentinels approach to developing a manufacturers ability to increase profits. They build high level commercial managers for their customers.

Working alongside them, helping develop programs to deliver top quality teams, has been an interesting world to live in.

They challenge themselves continually to keep it in the real world. If it doesn't work "out there" it doesn't belong in their classroom.

It has always amazed me that one of the big international retail companies has not written Dave a huge check to go sit on a beach somewhere and drink cocktails for the rest of his life. By my reckoning Sentinel has taken billions of dollars out of retailers pockets and put them back into manufacturers budgets.

On the other side of the coin they have added massive cash value to retailers too by developing better consumer strategies with their manufacturing customers.

So these guys are good, really good.

But their existence sparks another annoyingly simplistic question. If Category Management is working so well that retailers and suppliers can make more money taking warm showers together (metaphorically speaking) then why do we need Dave's business at all.

It's simple. In the time I have worked alongside Dave and his team it has become apparent that true, long term collaboration is a mere fantasy.

Yes, from time to time, it is in both companies interest to work extremely closely together but, ultimately, one thing overrides the partnership. Self interest.

Let's stay with simple ideas. What is a retail buyer or category manager paid to do? It's that easy. Make profit for the retailer.

What is a salesperson for a supplier paid to do? Exactly the same for their company. Two people doing the same job staring at the same pile of cash

That Game has been going on for the last 150,000 years.

So enter the hero, Category Management!

It's now no longer about who gets a share of the pie but how big can we make the pie.

Big pies for everyone! No more fighting over the crumbs.

Pies are not infinite though and sooner or later the pie stops growing and may even shrink. The need for more profit doesn't. This naturally happens in times of recession.

Yes, Category Management is needed to change the recipe, as tastes change over time, but you still end up with two people staring at each other's plate thinking how can I get more of theirs. "They don't deserve that much, they can make do with less."

In 2008 Marks & Spencer, one of the UKs most respected retailers, hit the headlines. One of its top suppliers, Northern Foods, had announced that it was going to close a factory with the loss of 730 jobs.

The reason they gave was the breakdown in price discussions with M&S. But what makes this story very interesting is that the factory had been built 21 years before to make products for that retailer! 21 years in "partnership". Working together. Building a mutually successful business structure.

After all that time the break down in talks was not over one of the

Italian Ready Meals Northern Foods made for M&S. It was over the pie.

This is not an isolated incident where a long term partnership degrades due to money. It happens all the time.

As you read this there are suppliers in the offices of retailers around the world being told to improve pricing, lower cost, extend terms, increase marketing payments etc. The list goes on and on. This is why Dave and his team are kept very busy.

Why does this mean that Category Management has the odds stacked against its survival?

Because part of the process of buying products from a supplier or selling them to a retailer is negotiation.

Negotiation is poker. When you play poker do you trust the other players?

Category Management is built on trust and collaboration. This is why, in many companies now, the two things are being split apart. A Category Management team work on increasing the pie and a negotiation team slice it up.

So if self interest will ultimately erode the positive relationship required to make Category Management work, what can be done to fix the situation.

First and foremost we have to be honest about the world we live in. Self interest is necessary to protect the profits and long term success of the businesses we represent.

Our objective is, typically, to make more money tomorrow than you did yesterday.

Ok so if we know that the other person across the table has the same objective then we know we are playing the same game.

Now we have to accept that there may be an element of dishonesty or misrepresentation that occurs from time to time. It could just be that information is omitted.

However it happens we know that a retailer is never going to tell a manufacturer they accept lower margins from their competitors. We also know that a manufacturer will never tell a retailer that it's competitors products are really better than the ones they are trying to sell.

The technical term for this is lying.

Lying is a collaborative act. A lie only has power if the person being lied to chooses to believe it.

The only way that Category Management can be really effective is if we understand there is a complete difference between Category Management and negotiation. Too many times it feels like we are part of a positive exercise focused at increasing profits for everyone and, in actual fact, we are really in the middle of a negotiation designed to steel most of the pie.

So stage one of dealing with this is knowledge. Not just about the business. Yes, we need a clear understanding of how both retailers and manufacturers generate profits from shoppers and consumers.

The additional knowledge you need is that you are playing The Game. Always. And it will not stop.

To deal with this you must have the skills to know when the other party has their hand in your pocket and is about to steal your wallet.

You also need to know how to deal with this when it happens without destroying the opportunity to generate long term profit through collaboration.

It's pointless getting upset when it happens, they are just doing their job. What we need to be able to do is re focus both parties on the larger opportunities that await you. You must be able to integrate top level negotiation skills into the Category Management process if it is ever going to work in real life.

If you want to know how to do this successfully I suggest you give someone like Dave a call. He will, for a modest fee, help you build a level of judgement as to what you are facing, how to integrate it with Category Management skills and how to deal with behaviour driven by self interest.

Without this clear understanding of the realities of the business environment we live in collaboration through Category Management, to deliver long term profit for all, can only ever be a theoretical exercise.

This is because it is built on part truths, misrepresentations and filtered insights.

7 SIGNS OF LIFE
OR
"WHAT A 10 YEAR OLD CAN TEACH YOU ABOUT RETAILING"

It seems that I have painted an extremely dark picture of the retail world we are all part of and the difficult pressures it lives under. A dangerous place where lies and deceit are part of everyday life.

Is retailing descending into a culture of "make certain the right product is on the correct shelf, in the optimum location at a competitive price and make it look good"?

Has innovation, real innovation, died?

The reality is that there are signs of life out there.

My 10 year old son James hit the nail on the head. We are both very lucky and have the chance to travel around the world together to some of the most amazing cities on the planet.

When we walk a store together he is used to looking at it from a merchandising perspective. He can see things on a store walk that many shop managers will miss.

I wanted to see retail through the eyes of a 10 year old because their motivation is so simplistic. The natural human desire for acquisition is at its most un-diluted at that age. "I want everything I can see and I want it yesterday" is their mantra.

When I asked him the question "which store, anywhere in the world that you have been, would you like to go back to the most?" I was startled by the answer.

It should strike fear into the heart of every retailer out there. He said he "would prefer the internet"!

This is a child who has been to Hamleys in London. A multi story extravaganza of toys and games, all of which are within reach and most can even be played with.

He said "it's easier to find what I like on the internet. Finding it yourself in a store was a pain, the internet finds it for you".

"In a store you do not know if they have it. The internet always does."

A retail store can never beat the range and distribution the internet has. The main restriction to using it are the logistics, which create convenience issues. When that is solved, and believe me it will be at one time by someone far smarter than me, the game will change again.

It has already started in the UK.

To explain why the UK should be at the cutting edge of route to consumer strategies I need to introduce an old friend of mine. A really old friend. Really, really old. Andrew Thompson has spent large parts of his career developing, managing and evaluating the sales and route to consumer strategies for companies such as PepsiCo. He describes the FMCG environment facing manufacturers today as the most challenging he has seen in his career and it's getting harder.

He currently works with huge international businesses in all parts of the world and views the UK as one of the most developed and toughest retail environments for manufacturers sales and logistics teams to work in.

Napoleon famously stated "L'Angleterre est une nation de boutiquiers." The direct translation is "England is a nation of shopkeepers" and it is as true today as it was then.

Getting the product from the factory to the consumer while minimising costs and maximising speed is an art form in itself. Andrew has had to use mixtures of distributor, direct to store, wholesale, van sales and any other legitimate means to get his products, and now his customers products, into the hands of a consumer.

Having worked on distributor management projects with him in Asia, the Middle East, Europe, the USA, and the former Soviet Union, I can say he has enough experience to make a valued judgement on which markets are the most challenging. So when he tells me to look at the UK as an indicator of changes in distribution strategy I take his advice seriously.

So how is the UK adapting to the new world we are retailing in? Shutl is a great example. If you are shopping on line and see the Shutl logo you will have the opportunity to get same day delivery for a ridiculously low price, sometimes even free. How does this work? They developed a network of couriers, sometimes exploiting their downtime between other deliveries, to get the purchased product to the consumer when they want it i.e. now.

As I am typing this I have their website open and they are quoting the shortest delivery time so far as 13 minutes 57 seconds! And this is just the start.

The fact that there is a demand for companies like Shutl shows you that, as markets develop, the barriers to Internet sales will fall away. The whirlwind is about to sweep away preconceptions about the reach of e-tailing.

Even in categories such as clothing, technological solutions to sizing differences will appear in the next few years.

I look forward to downloading an App from Levi's onto my iPhone 100 which uses the on board laser reader to 3D model my body. It will then send it to the online store where an automated fabrication unit will immediately produce the perfect 501s for me. The App will then send same 3D model to Grand Theft Auto where it constructs a virtual me to live out the fantasy gangster life I always thought I should have chosen. And I will be wearing my new 501s.

Back in the now, I still wanted more information from my son James on what a 10 year old loves in a store.

I asked him why he didn't want to order his M&Ms on line? Instead he wanted to go to M&M World in Las Vegas when we were in town?

Why? Because he had fun. It made him feel happy! Eating the sweets was not the need that was satisfied. He wanted to enjoy himself.

His life was better not because of the product but because of the experience of acquiring it.

"It was like a theme park" he said.

Multiple floors, live character meets, a mini movie theatre, full size race car, personalised M&Ms and, of course, all the associated merchandising products. As I am writing this I am drinking my coffee out of a mug with a smiling, red M&M on its side.

To a 10 year old it feels like an interactive experience which enriches his emotional existence. And while he is getting high on life he also buys some products.

M&M world is not a sweet shop. Most children do not go there primarily to buy candy. It is there to deliver fun. It does, however, make its profits by selling sweets and merchandise to those people enjoying themselves inside its walls.

On the strip in Vegas they could have hung a giant sign saying "Cheapest sweets in town!"

Would that have made them destination?

They also might mention "Biggest selection in town!" Could that have built the amazing footfall that they enjoy?

None of these can ever deliver what this store does. Thousands of smiling faces every day that belong to people who have had their pockets emptied buying a category which is typically an impulse product.

The product is still an impulse sale. The people flock through the door in droves because their primary objective is to feel and specifically to feel good. That is what the store is destination for.

If you are a retailer or manufacturer and want to be challenged to be great not just ok. To be part of the future not a relic of the past. To be an important part of people's lives not just an interchangeable "me too" then Las Vegas is an excellent place to learn your trade.

Apart from the obvious sensory inputs they have there, and I will come back to a few of them, you have another retailing game changer located in town. Bass Pro Shops.

They have an edge of town location that any person who has ever imagined themselves "surviving the end of civilisation as we know it" will love.

It is essentially a sporting goods chain. That simple. It specialises in products for hunting and fishing. Sounding sexy yet? I thought not.

Many of the products can be bought in a giant Kmart.

What you can't get in the main stream competitors is this. You don't get a massive outdoor and indoor area full of boats.

You don't get an indoor area where you can get fly fishing lessons.

Likewise you wouldn't expect a gun range, where you can try out your purchases, behind the display of hunting riffles.

The place is littered with giant glass tanks where you can go eye to eye with live examples of the fish you could catch. I can now see a huge fish in front of me and in my mind I know I will catch one just like it in a struggle worthy of a book by Hemingway. I just need to buy the right products and get some good advice from experts. Hey, that's handy, I'm in a store that can do both of those things.

I saw a Bass Pro Shop sign near Miami years ago. I didn't know it then, but I had already become a customer of theirs. I just hadn't bought anything yet.

When I spent a couple of weeks in Vegas I thought "I have to go to a Bass Pro Shop if there is one in town". To this day I still do not know why I have such a strong affinity with the brand. I think it may have something to do with the fact that I was brought up in the country and my memories as a child of happy days fishing with friends are brought swimming back as I walk into the stores. Survival skills in the wild have always interested me.

The reality is that I live near Geneva in Switzerland and the hardest decision I have to make about survival is do I risk another Fondue for lunch given the dangers of cholesterol at my age?

Anyway I know it is not because I need to catch fish to eat. Unlike our 150,000 year old ancestor who invented retailing, I can still go to Anymart and buy my fresh Scottish Salmon even when I am 3000 miles away from the waters in which they were caught.

Why do I need to shop at a store where they can equip you to take on any environment?   It's simple. I like it. I buy clothes that are totally over specified for the use they get from me.

As my son stares into a cabinet of knives, I tell him the same thing my dad told me when I was his age, "A knife is a tool not a weapon" and it makes me feel good. My father died a long time ago and, yes, I still miss him. At Bass Pro Shop I remember how much. Looking around me at other fathers and sons I know they will feel the same in the future.

I purchase fishing gear and imagine I am "The old man and the sea" even though I catch the equivalent of the bait he would use.

"Me, an amateur?   No, I shop at Bass Pro Shops".   I buy

credibility at Bass Pro. When I visit an Anymart I check in the sporting goods section. Try as I might I have never found credibility on a shelf. Perhaps they are out of stock? I blame the logistics team.

It is not a coincidence that people choose to shop at Bass. It is THE place they want to spend their time and their money but not because it is cheaper. Yes customers expect value but that is not what makes it The Place To Buy.

There are not many stores in which you suddenly find yourself surrounded by a pride of lions as you walk next to a waterfall. Then, within seconds, you can be surrounded by a school of fish hanging in the air around you.

To real sportsmen and women the store places them in scenes where they use the products they can buy. To enthusiastic wannabes like me, who may enjoy using some of their products camping with my son, I want to enjoy using something a pro would use.

I drive a Jeep. It's goes off road about twice a year. Why don't I buy a BMW X5? Because a pro wouldn't drive one. It can easily handle what I would use it for but not what a pro needs. So it's not for me.

We are sliding towards that ice covered lake called brand equity and values.

Product marketeers, especially in the luxury sector, have understood for years the emotional value of an item can far outweigh its cost.

Take, for instance, Louis Vuitton. It is difficult to compare buying this weeks special offer of yogurt to the, near sexual excitement, of a woman buying her first LV. It is nothing to do with how beautifully the product is crafted. You would not expect anything less.

Typically what she is buying is status within her social group. "If I have so many resources, I can afford to waste them on a bag, you can only guess how successful and, therefore, desirable I am".

Luxury product manufacturers often carry the weight of

delivering purchasing excitement for retailers. The thought of owning your first Rolex is so great that a retailer would have to go a long way to turn that shopping trip into a boring and painful experience. It doesn't stop them trying sometimes. Take, for instance, the arrogant shop assistant in an upmarket clothing store that stares at your Converse Allstars in a way that says "if you are wearing those you can't afford to shop here".

In store theatre goes hand in hand with high ticket, luxury goods. It also sits well with Perfume and Cosmetics. Many department stores do a good job by offering a free makeover and advice for customers. Unfortunately this is also a strategy that can be copied. In store demonstrations provide, what many retailers like to call excitement and theatre. It is interesting they use this terminology.

I pay money for tickets to go to a theatre and be excited. Would I pay for tickets to your store? If the answer is yes you can tick the box. If it's no stop your teams using the words or change things. We can come back to this later.

Let's go back to our friends at Bass Pro Shop. How do they provide excitement and theatre while differentiating themselves. They draw on other ideas, not just the imitation savannahs in their Vegas store.

On the drive from Miami to Key West I stopped at another of their outlets. This format is the World Wide Sportsman and focuses, more specifically, on the market for fishing.

If you ever go to The Keys you will understand why. It's a fisherman's paradise. Mile after mile of beautiful ocean front and waterways to fish from and if you get bored with that, head to sea. The waters that surround the string of linked islands seem as deep as forever, run all the way to Cuba and are the hunting ground for some of the most amazing sport fish on the planet.

So you would expect the Bass Pro store at Illamorada to be pretty impressive. It is. Yes you have all the tackle any person would ever want. It has range depth and width to die for. Professionals and amateurs are catered to with products for every budget.

It even has the sister boat to Hemingway's famous "Pilar" taking centre stage in the middle of the sales floor. Yes, that's what I said. A full size, ocean going boat taking up the space you could use for gondolas with more product.

Where does that fit with a Category Management Planogram produced by a "Category Captain"? I don't think Hemingway, a man amongst men, would see too many manufacturers wearing an invisible Cap and Badge as capable Captains of "Pilar".

Soon we will move towards taking the helm of Retail Shopper Management. How can we share a responsibility in the success of our businesses given that the sands, on which we have built our world, are shifting?

At one time the threat of the e-tailing competitors looked like it spelt the end for traditional bricks and mortar retailers. That was never true. All they ever did was show how fragile purely price, quality, convenience retailing was.

What will kill stores on the high street, malls and out of town is boredom. Plain and simple. They will be less than what is coming next. The tornado is touching down and you can see this nowhere better than when you are dining out.

Talk about sensory input!

Music, taste, texture, light, scent. They have it all and through these they deliver emotional attachment.

How many times have you heard someone say "I love this restaurant because..."

This is in stark comparison to a large format food store. It's not often people use the word love in conjunction with one of them, although their marketing teams dream of it happening.

The "because" is normally followed by things like:
I celebrated my birthday there and it was wild.
I sang with the band. I still can't believe I did it.
I met my husband there.

The food makes me feel soooooo bad it's that good.

I feel I am one of the locals.

They are so happy to see me.

It is a home away from home.

The owner is the most miserable man on earth. You have to meet him, he's great!

You won't believe how much the kids enjoy it there.

They have the most amazing...   ...memorabilia, music, merchandise, display of...

It keeps on going.   We have five senses that stimulate all our emotions. Restaurants cater to them all.

So let's head back to the Bass Pro Shop at Illamorada. What do you think they do to maximise the sensory input in the land of fantasy fishing. A restaurant? Not just any restaurant. They have the "World Famous Illamorada Fish Company".

This is about as far away from an Anymart cafe as you can get. It also doesn't have the ridiculous low price and random product names that Swedish retailer Ikea has to offer which keep footfall high.

No, the "World Famous Illamorada Fish Company" is so different. Yes the food is a mixture of traditional American main stream menus plus local specialities. Try the ribs. Your taste buds will love you forever and the margaritas! Oh momma!

What it has that makes this place special is the location. It is built over the ocean. In the small lagoon where it sits you can see giant Tarpon swim underneath you. You look out onto the ocean and know the fish you order for lunch may have been in the same water that morning.

It is open air and built like a giant wooden beach hut.

The staff are spectacular. The live music is brilliant.

But you know what. I can hear the cries of retailers saying "but you can't expect us to compete with that location!"

No I don't. Because you are not the management at Bass. They didn't have the African savannah in Las Vegas but they built it because that's what made their shoppers feel something.

They knew it was the right thing to do because it felt right.

Bass Pro Shops' mission statement:

"To be the leading merchant of outdoor recreational products, inspiring people to love, enjoy, and conserve the great outdoors."

Love. Enjoy. Conserve.

Not a price message in sight. They know it is a given that prices have to be competitive. That quality has to be 100%. That customer service and stock availability has to happen.

Love. Enjoy. Conserve.

I once (or twice) got caught for speeding when I was younger. As I was a teenager at the time it had a significant impact on me and I remember the first conversation in detail.

It was especially memorable because the typical English police officer completes an advanced course in caustic, quick wit with a masters in sarcasm.

Me: "was I doing something wrong officer?"

Police Officer: "trying to escape earths gravitational pull I believe sir".

Me: "sorry, I am normally a good driver."

Police Officer as he looks at the numerous dents and scratches on my first car: "Really? Rent a wreck is it?"

Me, now indignant about the abuse my wonderful set of wheels was receiving. " Look, I wasn't trying to get caught for speeding".

His next words were the same words I would offer to any retailer writing their mission statement and including value, price, quality, customer service and satisfaction.

He leaned into my face and said "you don't need to state the bleeding obvious sir".

Go to www.google.com and put in the following words. "Mission statement" and then add your favourite FMCG multinational food retailer. You will see what I mean.

So did I buy anything on this visit to Bass? No. I bought everything! Rods, reels, tackle, the works. But what I actually bought was a unique experience I wanted to share with my son. I bought a memory. Bass Pro Shops put it in front of me within reach and I grabbed it with both hands.

Taking my son ocean fishing for the first time is something I will never forget. Seeing his face when he caught a Barracuda was spectacular.

But here is the amazing thing. The store involved my wife in the experience too. So much so that she came away with a pink fishing rod of her own. Yes pink, I jest you not. This is a person who may get excited about many things in life but fishing is about as far away from any of them as you can get.

She did not buy a fishing rod because it was a great price, although it had a bearing on which one she bought, she did it because she wanted to be part of the family experience.

To belong.

Bass Pro Shops' mission statement:

"To be the leading merchant of outdoor recreational products, inspiring people to love, enjoy, and conserve the great outdoors."

Tick the box Bass Pro Shops, you can go for a beer to celebrate a job well done!

8 RETAIL SHOPPER MANAGEMENT
OR
"THE HELLS ANGELS GUIDE TO DELIVERING RETAIL MAGIC"

During the middle of the last century, post World War II, biker clubs started to spring up throughout the United States. Many of these clubs were described as gangs in the press.

Urban legend grew up around incidents, now famous in American history, concerning their violent clashes between each other and police.

On the 4th of July 1947, at a little town called Hollister in California, the American Motorcyclist Association had sanctioned an event throughout the holiday weekend.

Motorcyclists and clubs flooded the town in their thousands for a weekend of partying.

This was far more than anticipated and caused a doubling of the local population with the associated problems that might be expected.

Over the next few days, fights and drunkenness hit the streets of Hollister.

It was dubbed the "Hollister Riot" by the media, even though it was relatively low level in comparison to a real city riot. Some locals even said the bikers were not really doing anything bad.

News of the incident spread, however, and gave members of the public grave concerns about the menacing nature of these "biker gangs".

The American Motorcyclist Association were rumoured to have responded by saying "the trouble was caused by the one per cent deviant that tarnishes the public image of both motorcycles and motorcyclists" although this has never been substantiated.

Interestingly some biker clubs responded by using the 1% insignia to describe themselves.

The outcome of all this notoriety was that many people were instantly suspicious or fearful of bikers. Some individuals inside the clubs even became targets of violence themselves at times.

The response to this by the clubs was very simple and has worked for them ever since.

If you are a Hells Angel, for instance, and you see one of your club members being attacked for any reason, it is expected that you will stand shoulder to shoulder with them, regardless of the odds.

"One in, all in" is a strategy that has meant that you really have to think twice before you take on any member of their club. If you take on one, you take on all. Strength is delivered through complete, unwavering commitment to the group regardless of the personal risks involved.

So what has this got to do with making a quantum leap in the direction of a new level of consumer and shopper engagement?

Retail Shopper Management is a commitment that steps beyond a retailers or manufacturers own walls. It has to do with both signing up to a single, over arching aspiration, to make an impact on an individuals life. A real impact.

It is completely different to Category Management in that it focuses on, not only the experiential requirement of an individual outside the basic needs satisfied by a product sector, but also their emotional needs and desires.

What the impact to a persons life is depends on the area where your business is targeted. It also depends on the ability to be creative and produce value from the endeavour.

Low levels of current margin in a business are no excuse for not delivering a new experience or benefit to your customers.

Indeed, in many instances, the benefit to you may well be that the person enjoying this new, positive feeling, will actually be the customer of a competitor. This adds significant value to a retailer if it creates real loyalty not just loyalty through geographical convenience.

The key to this process, and the commonality with the Hells Angels, is that you have to have a "one in, all in" approach.

Manufacturers and retailers have to share the same vision of what they can bring to peoples lives. It is pointless for a retailer, presenting a direction which provides shoppers with an element of care free fun for instance, if it cannot be supported by a manufacturers products and promotions.

Retail Shopper Management steps beyond Category Management and starts with a re writing of a companies mission.

Most retail mission statements are about delivering the ticket to the show.

Price, quality, value, best for less, customer centric, delivering great service etc.

Lets have a new rule, if it is a given in a market place that you have to be competitive on price and deliver customer satisfaction, get it out of the mission statement.

Otherwise you have just lowered your ambition to produce the same as the next guy.

And I need to be very clear, this is not the usual, low level, vague, unexciting and trite mission statement that every marketeer is trained to produce when they exit university. It should have teeth, commitment and consequences.

Increase ambition and focus on what you are there to do.

I have a simple example of this and it comes from, I am sorry to say, Apple.

The reason I am disappointed to be mentioning them is that they are just over exposed in books about business.

But here I am about to use them as a great example of what I am trying to get at. So much for original writing!

Published in 2013, Apple released a new advert that described what the company was there to achieve for their customers and for people they hoped would eventually become their consumers. It didn't focus on cutting edge technology, nor on increasing processor speed and delivering smarter devices.

It showed the direction and difference Apple has to many of its competitors. If you want to see the add google "Designed by Apple" and you will find the video. Its very impressive. Here is the text:

"If everyone is busy making everything, how can anyone perfect anything? We start to confuse convenience with joy, abundance with choice. Designing something requires focus. The first thing we ask is: What do we want people to feel? Delight. Surprise. Love. Connection. Then we begin to craft around our intention. It takes time... There are a thousand no's for every yes. We simplify. We perfect. We start over. Until everything we touch enhances each life it touches. Only then do we sign our work: Designed by Apple in California."

Emotion driving design? Interesting focus. The reason I use this as an example is what they say at the beginning of the ad. "We start to confuse convenience with joy, abundance with choice". I absolutely see their point. Look at many FMCG grocers.

I came across the advert by chance as I started to write this chapter. It paraphrases many ideas in the first part of this book. Isn't it irritating when a person can get an idea over in a few lines but it takes you many pages.

Compare Apples' mission to one of their biggest rivals, Samsung. Their vision and mission to 2020 is:
"Inspire the world, Create the future".

How are they going to achieve this? They want "To inspire the world with innovative technologies, products and designs that enrich peoples lives".

So, if I follow the logic, if Samsung produce innovative technologies it will inspire the world.

Apple want people to feel emotions. To do this they "craft" products.

Samsung create innovative technologies which they believe will then inspire people.

Emotion delivering the outcome vs technology delivering the outcome.

Both very aspirational in the way they want to affect a consumers world, both very different.

It seems a bit chicken and the egg but, in truth, it shows some of the fundamental differences in ideology between the two organisations. Each business is amazingly successful, the question is, which one has a more sustainable competitive advantage?

Only time will tell. For my part I hate Apple products. I have always been a Windows person. Being able to get behind the facia of a computer program gives me a greater sense of control. Apple always seems too constricted and difficult to tinker with.

So that being the case, why am I writing this book on an iMac and an iPad while listening to music on my iPhone? Because the Mac makes me smile when I use it. My Sony Vaio never did. The iMac is just beautiful. End of.

Yes it works seamlessly when I pick up my iPad, open this manuscript, and it automatically syncs. But it is the way it makes me feel that made me switch allegiance not its functionality.

So getting back to vision and mission statements for retailers, what emotion could you insert into a mission statement that would change the way you approach shopper interaction? How could your suppliers join in with this and align themselves to how you produce promotions for instance. Would it engender a "one in, all in" environment that manufacturers voluntarily commit to.

We are used to analysing performance and shopper behaviour in a category to establish an opportunity gap for a product. Why not look at it from a different point of view. Are there any opportunity gaps in your sector of the market for feeling a positive emotion while shopping? For instance how many shoppers in yours and your competitors stores laugh out loud because they are enjoying the shopping experience so much? If the answer is none you now have a possible performance gap to fill which could give you an edge in the market.

Now that's a crazy KPI isn't it. No longer do you have to judge yourself by on shelf availability because it's a must have. It will never go away so it has to happen and be reported on. Instead you can measure the success of your strategy with the L.P.H. quotient. Laughs Per Hour.

Ok, you may now be thinking "Mark has lost the plot and I have wasted a few hours of my life reading this book in the desperate hope that it may provide me with some ideas for change". But think about it for a minute. What is missing from your range and distribution? Nothing really.

Category Management has done a good job for the past 20 years and that means the opportunity for growth is minimal in relative terms. It is not loyal though. Category Management works for all your competitors. Small increments are possible but they are available to all within a short period. Nobody likes disloyalty. People have been killed over less. Perhaps this could be a motive for its demise? We will see.

But if Category Management is not creating divergence, what is the thing that can step change the market and polarise shoppers to one geographic location and retailer? This is the question. But the answer also has to be sustainable and difficult to copy.

So back to the Hells Angels approach to retailing. If, as a retailer, you make a crazy decision and decide to be known as the fun place to shop (and by the way the prices are always great) then do you think you could align your suppliers behind that?

Can you have a "one in, all in" approach to achieving the objective and share that commitment with your suppliers. Will they reflect your commitment? If the answer is no then it may mean that the time, effort and cost will be prohibitive.

And what about a manufacturer. If you say your piece in the puzzle is to deliver excitement, for instance, you might say you are already doing it but be honest with yourselves.

Excitement will not happen by launching a new flavour of potato chips. You may think Spicy Armadillo flavour crunchy tortillas, in a new convenient size pack, is the most amazing thing to hit the salty snack aisle this year. It may well test market better than your competitors Peppered Beaver flavour tortillas but, in reality, it is probably only truly exciting for the teams in R&D or Marketing. It will not be for a potential consumer or shopper.

Ask a shopper what the last thing that really made them excited was and it will not be anything as mundane as a product or end gondola display. It will be a date with a new lover, booking a holiday somewhere special or perhaps their sons first performance in his rock band at school. A "new flavour" of this and a "limited edition" of that is as exciting as finding fluff in your navel. It's different, not exciting.

Perhaps excitement needs a better definition because retailers and manufacturers have a conflicting view to consumers and shoppers.

How about this. ***Excitement is something that triggers a deep felt emotion or physical reaction***, like laughing or crying for instance.

We can call it the OMG factor. If shoppers stop and say "oh, my god!" then we can assume we can tick the excitement box.

The aspiration to create an OMG retailing environment should not just be limited to the city centre and flagship stores. Everyone deserves it. So many times I have visited some really good stores in strategic locations which get the flagship makeover. Some are near a retailers head office and are therefore just convenient for the team to get to. Others showcase their wares to potential investors.

In the meantime the other eighty percent of the estate are left to deliver a completely different experience for shoppers.

I was recently in Geneva and visited the Manor store. Manor are an upmarket department store combined with FMCG food hall.

They really make a great job of creating theatre in each of the food categories. A bakery that you virtually walk through producing beautiful smells, spectacular butchers preparing fantastic, mouthwatering meals right in front of you. Seafood to die for arranged with the artistic flair of Andy Warhol. Ready cooked food that would shame some top class restaurants. Yes I was very hungry the day I walked the store.

In contrast to this, the other stores they have just outside Geneva are adequate but, in no way, deliver the mouth watering experience this one does. They are similar like an own brand tomato sauce is similar to Heinz but, as my son tells me, it's just not the same.

Black and white movies vs 3D with full Dolby surround sound. The experience is just bigger.

Larger space does provide a greater ability to produce some of this theatre and higher footfall creates more conversion opportunities but ultimately it can only be an excuse to think you cannot achieve theatre in a small space.

I just want to digress for a second. When we talk about in store theatre I, again, would like to get some clarity on what is meant.

To most people a theatre in the real world is made up of the building, a stage, actors and a story to be told. If all this combines together well the audience becomes emotionally involved with the whole event and, ultimately, leave feeling they have been entertained.

So if we translate this into retail terms, the building is the store, the stage is the shop floor, the actors are products and the stories are the promotional mechanics that tell shoppers whats going on and involve them personally to the point where they buy.

This is why spot lights are trained on products in shops to create luminous pools within the store the same same way actors are lit by spot lights and the audience remains in subdued lighting.

Everything is in place for a great piece of theatre. If our audience leaves the building thinking they have been entertained as well as supplied product we can therefore say we have created in store theatre.

If not, we cannot make that statement. This is an interesting idea to have in your head when you walk a store and view the execution against a more testing set of standards.

These statements we make about excitement, engagement, theatre are brilliantly aspirational words but if we do not have a clear, honest and ambitious view of what they look like it only cheapens our offer.

Allowing teams to casually throw these words around without challenging them against real peoples expectations does not help anyone.

When you walk a store as a retailer or manufacturer ask the following:

Have I enjoyed the experience so much I would pay a little extra for the privilege?
Was I taken on a journey at some point?

Did I learn anything new about myself?

How many times was I stopped in my tracks and literally wowed? OMG!

If I hadn't bought anything was it still a worthwhile use of my time being in the store?

Have I the urge to put something on a social network raving about my trip and it isn't about a product?

Probably the question now is how can we start to move towards a retailing format that is defensible, different and delivers?

So stage one of Retail Shopper Management is, first and foremost, to set a strategic direction to the business that is outside the traditional format that delivers a me too result.

It is worthwhile, at this point to introduce another person who can significantly help everyone look at things in a different way. Dr Dan Herman heads up the Think Short network and is author of "Outsmart the MBA Clones". He is brilliant at challenging businesses to be unique.

I share Dr Herman's opinion that strategies are not born out of data analysis, they are born out of a creative process. If we develop a strategy based on data alone we will be mirroring what is happening in all your competitors because they have been taught the same way. Same universities, same business schools, same results within a narrow band. In fact I personally do not think it matters if it is a vision, a mission, a strategy or an objective. Yes I know that runs counter to everything we hear in large corporations but it is more important that it is real, becomes part of our everyday business and is actioned continuously. Actually you just have to do something, anything is better than inertia, but once committed you must live it. And when I say inertia I actually mean competitive inertia. Retailers and manufacturers in developed markets are moving forward at roughly the same speed as their competitors when measured over the mid term. Sometimes one moves faster than the others but then competitors catch up or overtake the growth rate. This is often because everyone is using the exact same gap analysis for their business.

What does good look like?
Where do we measure against this?
What do we have to change to get there?

The first and most common mistake people make is assuming they have a handle on what good looks like. Good is normed by the traditional development path for managers. This combined with a mathematical analysis of data to derive a strategy will deliver the same results.

The first thing that has to change is that part of the process which defines the outer boundaries of our ambition and imagination. I quite like Dr Herman's solution:
What's happening now?
What's possible?
What's feasible and profitable?
What's next?

The what's possible element is the key. In a traditional analysis of what good looks like it is constrained by the boundaries we have created through experience and what the data tells us. Whats possible is based on a different creative approach that is outside typical strategic thinking. Read Dr Herman`s book, it will help explain. I do not want to spend time recreating it here.

Moving on. However you describe your challenge and direction it has to be different from what has gone before. No more wishful thinking mission and visions.

Some suggested criteria for this could be that:
It must not contain KPI's that are associated with providing what your competitors all provide as standard eg Every Day Low Prices.
Should include an emotion. How do you want people to feel when they shop in your store.
Mention how all of a shoppers five senses will be triggered to create the experience.
Could contain an element of natural disruption to avoid the concept becoming stale e.g. once a category, product, promotion or mechanic is deemed a success it is the mission of that team to destroy it and build something better.

It must be honest, not just created to tick a marketeers or investors box.

Must include a people element but not be a "leveraging our employees unique skills" babbling BS statement. Every employee knows that most major corporate companies would exit them in a heartbeat if it meant achieving the annual bonus so let's not blow smoke up their rear end. Tell it like it is. How about just "letting the team make one piece of magic happen everyday" or "listening to employees ideas with the same reverence we listen to consultancies".

It is ambitious and measurable not weak and vague. If you can't fail then it's not a stretch.

Describe what you add to a persons life which is not associated with value or quality.

So what will you, as a retailer, get from shifting your focus from the existing strategy to engaging retail customers in a more emotional way? You get the wholly grail of retailing. Loyalty.

When I see a FMCG retailers mission is to become the store in the hearts and minds of its customers it makes me wonder how they believe this is going to happen when the market place is becoming a zero degree game through the norming of competition.

Think back to the first time you fell in love. How did your body react inside (keep it clean people)? What went through your mind? Set that as the bar for how you want shoppers to feel about your stores, then you have a stretch target for the business.

But how can you do it? How can even a simple grocery store trigger a significant emotional response in shoppers.

First lets go back to the five senses. The first and primary one that retail overwhelms a shopper with is visual imagery. Stand outside or just in the entrance to a store and look to the back wall. Can you pick out key messages that make you want to buy a product or at least browse the category? Can you even see the back wall? If it`s just a sea of POS and giant gondolas it`s an instant fail.

Eye tracker analysis of shopper behaviour tells us where prime locations are to be found when customers enter a category or during dwell time at the cash desk but why can`t we be more ambitious?

In a superstore environment what stops us selling a product or category from 20 metres away? Research is mostly based in a traditional, gondola driven layout and ignores the emotional element. It is about delivery of information not delivery of an experience.

Lifestyle shots do not make people engage because they are wallpaper within todays media hailstorm.

Each category has its key messages to deliver to shoppers and this helps create this sea of information which camouflages the core messages of the store.

This needs to change if a store is to get a clear message across to shoppers as to what it is there to provide to someones life. As vision is the primary route to a persons mind it is imperative that messages are clear, distinct and not hidden by volume.

Even in fashion, luxury and electrical stores pretty displays are not the answer to the problem. Yes they may be aesthetically pleasing and show the product off well but what is the message the store is trying deliver? Does it even have one. Here is another simple tip. Work out and describe a stores personality within this environment. It helps suppliers and internal teams focus. You can use simple analogies from any environment to do it, for instance how about college? Is this store the nerdy but smart one, is it the coolest kid in the school? Maybe it`s the tough but sensitive rocker kid or the quirky, fun cheerleader? It really does not need to be complicated but the local environment should help dictate its style.

Fix the visual impact of the primary message a store needs to deliver and you have a foundation to move on to the next stage.

Product brands and retail brands can have dual representations. Dr John Medina, author of Brain Rules, has a brilliant input into how people make memories and then access them when required. His website www.brainrules.net is a treasure trove of information that can inspire retailers to think differently about how they engage with shoppers. In one section he talks about dual representations.

When the brain sees an object or symbol it starts to access memories the person has and connects the visual image to, not only what it is, but also to what it means to that person based on the input from previous experiences he or she has had.

Let me explain. Close your eyes and imagine a pair of women's red, high heeled, patent leather shoes. Now there is a picture in your mind because you have seen high heels before. You are recalling imagery that your brain has stored. Here is the question though, what does that image in your mind make you feel or remember? What is its meaning to you?

It may be an unusual thing to ask but the associations you make with an image or symbol will be built from inputs you have had throughout your life.

Humans are very good at utilising this ability, which is part of the theory of mind, to convey additional information including feelings.

This means that the most effective POS may not be the one showing the product. If you want to tap into a persons mind, and more importantly their feelings, you need to first ask how you want someone to feel so that you have the best chance of selling them something.

An easy example is hunger. How many times have you been grocery shopping and because you are hungry you leave with twice as many shopping bags as you normally would? This is why some retailers are now moving to high impact visuals that show food in its ready to eat format rather than the pack shot.

So if you want to cause someone to buy more, make them hungry first, but how can you expand this low level version into something much more impactful and emotional. How about something along the Disney advertising lines. Seeing a family, enjoy shared time preparing a meal together, could show how a retailers fresh produce area can have a more significant impact on people's lives. It could bring families together, create shared experiences and provide a platform for communication between generations.

Sounds a little out there? Stick with me, it's going to get crazier because it is starting to happen right now.

At the end of each year the drive for Christmas sales hits fever pitch. Over previous seasons, failures in how retailers have approached the market have wiped billions off their value. Market share, profit and stock value are all at risk. To make certain that major FMCG retailers in the UK get the chance to grab as much of the seasonal spend from the public, they pull out the big guns.

Massive TV advertising campaigns are launched which are closer to mini melodramas than to price off advertising. They hit the screens in sustained volume and get everyone talking about their favourites.

Social media is proliferated by comments suggesting which ones are the best and if they brought tears to the eyes as they played out visually beautiful scenes. They are all accompanied by perfect sound tracks aimed at engaging emotions at the deepest level.

If you would like to give your opinion try these:
John Lewis; The Bear and the Hare.
Tesco; Christmas TV advert 2013.
Marks and Spencer; Christmas fairytale 2013.

All of these are available on YouTube and are worth viewing back to back.

All of them keep the viewer engaged with exciting imagery and fantastic music. Both John Lewis and Tesco really pull at the heart strings with brilliant messages relating very little to their products or stores. All they want is the positive association with a real emotion that puts them front of mind during this period.

John Lewis even ran adverts advertising the upcoming adverts. OMG! They were that confident they were changing the game. Bets were being made that the soundtrack would be No1 in the Christmas charts.

Different to this is the Asda Walmart advert which shows how tough it is for mum at Christmas but the good news is Asda is on her side. Well done.

The last that I want to mention is Morrisons. Their Be Our Guest Christmas 2013 advert is completely different. Filled with product specific focus, service offers and value messages. All of this delivered by a dancing ginger bread man and with comedy presenters.

Watch all of them back to back and then decide for yourself which ones will be memorable in a few days time and which will still be talked about next Christmas.

Emotions embed messages far better than information. Now when I see a Tesco, John Lewis or Marks & Spencer store they have dual representations for me. I recall emotions and feelings which I experienced watching their adverts. They made me feel something and that is powerful.

The reason we have to consider how we can achieve this is because of the way we are built physiologically. If we want brand recall that says our Anymart store is good value then we don't need to change.

If, however, we want emotional recall not just factual recall about our stores we have to be different. Factual recall is often substitutional. "These guys are cheap, yes but these guys are cheaper".

Emotional recall is faster for our minds to remember and lasts longer so a retail store that has a dual representation, one as a credible grocery store and the other as a place which provides the ingredients and ideas to bring a family together is far more powerful in the struggle to achieve loyalty. It is also less substitutional.

If you really want to see some of the best advertising ever produced that attaches positive emotions to a relatively mundane type of business you should watch the adverts by TC Bank in Taiwan.

Their "Dream Rangers" and "Courage of Mother" visual masterpieces are also available on YouTube. Before you watch them think about a bank and write down a couple of words that you associate with it. Now watch the adverts and do the same for TC

Bank.

I have mentioned the Dream Rangers advert during some of my seminars and it never fails to bring tears to the eyes of many members of the audience.

So getting back to the Christmas bun fight for shopper share of pocket, how do the stores stack up against these highly uplifting adverts that represent their businesses? Do the stores take this emotional attachment through the line?

In most cases no. Yes there may be some visuals mirroring the mass media advertising but the reality people are faced with when they get to their local store is in stark contrast to the adverts. The magic disappears and reality brings you down to earth pretty quickly.

Having walked the stores of one of the producers of a magical advert mentioned above I can only describe them as shambolic. Massive queues at the tills, POS overload, confusing layouts, noise levels akin to sticking your head up the wrong end of a jet engine, non existent staff and a look closer to a tornado hit market stall than a world class retailer.

It is tragic.

Categories have their own agenda and this adds fuel to the fire that is burning the future of retail worldwide but what else can we do?

Lets take the "Family together cooking" theme forward and use it as a very basic example. If we want to trigger some emotional attachment we need to engage as many of the 5 senses as possible.

Why is this necessary? According to Brain Rules by John Medina a key element in recall is Multi Sensory Input. The more senses you stimulate, the longer the information is recalled.

So if you want people to recall how they felt during the advert, playing the associated soundtrack while viewing the images helps the person access the memories and feelings or, conversely, it can help embed them.

So if we have our our Family cooking together promotional space, which is highlighting this weeks suggestion, what sounds should people hear to help create or recall memories? I am certain you can be far more inventive than me but how about children and adults laughing? If it was the Sunday Breakfast promo week how about the sound of bacon sizzling in the pan?

Whatever you choose provides the opportunity to overlay two senses creating far greater impact.

Never underestimate the power of sound or music on the subconscious mind. A few years ago I spent some time in Orlando. As part of the trip we ended up in Universal Studios for a night out.

When you park the car it's in the multi-storey building connected to the Universal park. You have to walk through the garage and across a bridge to get to the entrance. I parked in the Jaws section, as you would, and we then started the 10 minute walk to the studio gates.

As we walked music played over the sound system.

It was background Muzak. It was Staying Alive by the BeeGees. It was brilliant!

I have a challenge for you. Download the track to your iPod, I know you don't have it already do you...   ...put on your ear phones and press play.

Now go for a walk.

30 seconds. That's all it takes and you can not avoid strutting to the music.

That's what happened at Universal. Hundreds of people started walking in unison and strutting. Everyone with a smile on their face. All, subconsciously, falling into the emotions generated from music they hear. Music connects to the soul. My generalisation not anyone else's.

I have sat in row 2 seat D, my favourite on short flights, and cried my eyes out to the music on my iPod. I am legendary now with certain crews as the emotional guy in row 2. Music is hard wired to feelings, emotions and memories. Fail to use it and it wastes a great opportunity to engage.

Ok, now we can move onto one of the most powerful senses of all, smell. Recalling information or emotions, while smelling the associated scent experienced when you first had them, can help you recover up to 50% more detail. This may be because smell has a direct access to the brain. Other senses do not.

So you can see where we are going with our fictional promotion. Yes we need to find someone who can create the smell of bacon frying unless we have a live cooking display. Unfortunately, I can tell you first hand, live cooking displays are not cheap and cannot run 24-7-365. A movement activated smell machine can and they are relatively low cost.

The good news is that there are companies out there producing them. If you want your candy section to smell of chocolate, your auto parts aisle to smell of new car and your diaper display to smell of… …well maybe this doesn't translate to some categories, but for the rest there are people who can achieve this for you in your stores.

Most grocery retailers are starting to handle the next sense well. Tasting products in key categories is becoming more prevalent although not as much as it is in parts of Asia. Try to do a tasting with a computer or smart phone and its going to get messy.

Sometimes, though, it still feels it is the focus in the top stores in many retail chains but not in the rest of the estate.

This gives the impression of a two class system for non focus or second tier stores. Don`t all shoppers, whatever their demographic or location, deserve a special experience when shopping?

Finally we are left with touch. Learning, which incorporates touch (Haptic), is important for many people. They get far more out of the process and they learn faster.

Why do you think that toy stores that have demonstrable displays do so well?

How can we get shoppers to physically engage with products in store? With some tastings like cheese and bread it is easy because they have to pick it up to eat it. With some others much harder but it is worth thought when we realise how important it is to overlay as many senses as possible. Even picking up a flyer for our fictional promotion, with cooking instructions for kids to follow instead of adults, helps a shopper engage better.

Ok, now we have a great promotional display which has impact at a deeper and more sustainable level but what is the x factor that is missing? It's the shopper. They provide the magic that makes it work. It is their memories that are triggered that provide the special ingredient in this process.

All their brain synapsis start firing bringing memories, feelings and emotions to their minds. Not a thought of how cheap it is but more how fun it is, how much everyone enjoys the moment they eat together and how simple things can be so rewarding. Get it right and they actively relive the moment in their minds while standing in front of your products.

This is a small step on the way to Emotional Retailing which is part of Retail Shopper Management and changes the fundamental way businesses engage with stores and products.

Retail Entertainment has been talked about, and delivered, by companies like Disney for decades now. But look back in history further. Traditional retailers at the turn of the last century have been peppered with individuals that entertained while selling products. From the tonic salesman in the covered wagon moving from town to town in the Wild West to Harrods in Knightsbridge which has been a wonderland for all ages since 1905.

Retailing was historically linked with sales and salesmanship. Many sales were assisted sales which enabled an element of interaction that was also an opportunity to entertain.

As businesses became larger, the ability to copy an entertaining style became more difficult and was replaced with quality, service, availability and price. In other words we just forgot how to do it. There was not a need because profits increased and, actually, it is not easy to do so why bother?

When all you need to be is a credible and local point of purchase it's a different game of securing locations, buying aggressively, maintaining quality and logistical expertise.

Now that my local point of purchase is in my pocket, it takes seconds to find the product and I can have it in my hands faster than if I drive to the store. The game has changed.

Retail Entertainment is not a new concept, it is an old skill humans have had which became outdated. But like many things it just needs the dust blowing of it and bringing up to date.

With many of these ideas, all we are doing is branding and compartmentalising fundamental forms of human interaction. If this is what you need for it to have credibility then let's call it Feel-Tailng, although it does sound slightly dodgy. As a retailer or manufacturer we are now in the business of selling feelings.

I personally prefer to keep it simple. Since mans early existence telling stories has been a significant part of social evolvement.

The reason it still remains part of our social DNA is because it feeds our emotions and excites our minds. And guess what, we are good at it. We use it to transmit information far beyond the words we use. Morality, concepts and ideologies can be explained through the use of stories far more easily than just providing information.

It seems sad that for decades now many of these skills have been lost in FMCG retailing and it is taking a shopper revolution to re-instil them in our high street.

Lets reclaim what was lost and it doesn't need a consultancy or a focus group to make it happen. The skills are in all of us, we just need to use common sense, get focused and remember how.

Time to move on, we have a mystery to solve.

9 SHOPPER AND CONSUMER METRICS
OR
A LESSON FROM A DEAD GIRL

Over the last ten years I have become more and more interested in Psychology and specifically how it affects the way people interact with each other and the world around them.

I have realised that it helps me understand different aspects of shoppers and consumers at a deeper level where it can help have a direct impact on how stores and products need to develop to be successful.

A key learning came by chance when I was researching the effect groups can have on an individual. To explain I have to retell a disturbing story and I apologise if it upsets anyone. It is well known and, so extensively reported that, it changed the way we view certain types of crowd behaviour.

At 3:15am on March 13th 1964, Catherine Susan "Kitty" Genovese arrived back at her apartment block in Queens, New York and parked her car 100 feet from the building. She had just finished her job managing a bar and was returning home.

As she closed the door of her car and headed out across the parking lot Kitty had no idea she only had just over an hour to live.

In the shadows Winston Moseley watched her and began to follow. Moseley would later confess that he had already killed and sexually assaulted two other women. Kitty realised something was wrong and began to run.

Before she could reach safety he caught her and stabbed her twice in the back. "Oh my God, he stabbed me! Help me!" Her desperate scream for assistance was heard by several residents but only a few realised that it was a cry for help.

One man shouted at Moseley to leave her alone and the attacker ran off but no one came to help Kitty.

She desperately tried to get into the building but a locked door prevented her access. Within a few minutes Moseley returned, searched for the injured girl and eventually found her.

Kitty fought back but was stabbed again and then sexually assaulted. A few minutes after the final attack one resident called the police and Kitty was taken to hospital at 4:15am. She succumbed to her wounds and died en route.

During the course of the investigations it was revealed that up to a dozen people saw or heard parts of the attack but few responded.

There was a public outcry at what was believed to be the apathy that was endemic within modern cities.

The incident eventually caught the attention of two researchers in the field of social psychology, John Darley and Bibb Lantané. They wanted to know why so many people failed to respond to the incident.

Their research is now famous and they have described the phenomenon as The Bystander Effect.

Simply put, they found that the probability of help is in reverse proportion to the number of bystanders. The more people, the less the chance for immediate help.

So why should this have any relevance on retail metrics? Let me explain.

Stage one of The Bystander Effect is that people in groups are less attentive to the world around them. Even in emergency situations groups recognise a threat more slowly than an individual.

This became apparent to me when working with the travel retail industry.

Airport retailers have an extremely unusual environment to work in. It allows them, if they want to, to measure key metrics such as shopper opportunity in cash and volume, shopper flow, footfall, conversion and basket size by day and even by hour if required.

Most FMCG retailers dream of these opportunities to understand how promotions, range changes and merchandising initiatives affect the core metrics of their business by location and to this level of detail.

It also causes some significant problems. Within an airport environment it is easy to realise you have a significant performance gap due to low footfall into store for instance.

If you realise this there are many ways that you can increase it but there is one that trumps the rest. When airports are refurbished the knee jerk reaction is to turn the store into a walk-through which means every passenger has to pass through to get to the gates.

The location is often just after security.

I want to offer one of the simplest ways for salespeople to make a success of dealing with retailers. Spend a lot of time in store watching and talking to potential shoppers. Have your meetings there. If you really want to be great why not offer to work in a different store once a quarter? There is no better way to understand how it all works. Chris Onslow my old CEO would applaud this statement.

You can't understand retail from a spread sheet, market share data or consumer insight. Go to the coal face and watch and, more importantly, count.

I spend time looking at stores and the way people interact with them. I watch them walking past stores, walking into stores, visiting categories, picking up products and then buying them. I am a shopper stalker.

The thing is every store has a personality. To understand how that personality affects shoppers you have to see it in action and count the positive and negative interactions to gain insight.

So what did I learn about walk-through stores that made me associate it with the terrible story of Kitty Genovese? It was the way shoppers reacted to the store. They passed through security and by the time they had made certain they had their phone, wallet, coat, handbag, purse they were a quarter of the way through the store.

Suddenly they became aware they were in a store. Because they were following the groups flow, and had low levels of consciousness about their surroundings, they did not realise their path took them through a shop.

Airports are also different because they put people under unnatural pressure. They are time challenged due to walk times, security checks and non standard layouts and this means that travellers often feel stressed in these environments.

I have seen some walk-through stores that create the "where am I look" on peoples faces closely followed by the "where do I have to go"? They don't create a "good I'm in a shop" look.

Because of this it makes it difficult to get shoppers to engage with the store. It is unlikely a shopper will walk back to the start so opportunities are lost.

They do not consider the store and products as relevant to them at this moment. What they have to offer does not meet an acknowledged current need which is critical for a person to satisfy.

A lack of consideration for a store is not limited to airports, it affects all retail stores. Wether the consideration works in the virtual construct a shopper builds in their mind before leaving on a purchase trip or inside the store when deciding wether to visit a category. Low level consideration can have many causes but whatever they are it needs a completely different solution than a lack of footfall does.

This was the key learning I took away. Shoppers have to consider the store as credible and more importantly relevant to themselves. Understanding that Consideration is a key metric is very important. It can be very easy to look at the numbers and believe a low frequency of visit is responsible for underperformance when, in actual fact, it is a low level of consideration that is causing the issue. You can end up viewing the symptom as the cause.

Shoppers also have to be able to counterbalance any effort that has to be expended against what they receive in return for consideration to occur. This can be achieved in several ways. An example is mathematically "it is such great value it is worth browsing". It can also be achieved emotionally "this was so much fun maybe I should buy something as a keep sake."

People go through clear stages as they move from a completely passive state to finally purchasing a product.

The stages are:
Disinterest. They see no relevance between the store and their current or future needs.
Consideration. The store is thought to be a potential point of purchase for products or services that may meet a need. This may manifest itself by people beginning to browse.
Active shopping. The person has direction and intent to buy.
Decision. Products are selected for purchase.

Moving people through these stages may only take a millisecond if products, that the individual buys as a daily staple, can be made visible. In most airports duty free stores the key product is tobacco. Adult smokers treat tobacco products as a daily staple and, because of ultra high brand loyalty and competitive price, moving a smoker through the four stages can be as easy as making the products visible at front of store.

This may not help in a walk-through store. Due to the Bystander

Effect potential customers may pass the category before they realise what has happened. It therefore occurred to me that the real challenges for any store are the following.

How can I show a potential customer that I am relevant to them?

How can I be unique enough to be considered as a point of purchase?

Critically, what do I need to do to switch a person from Consideration to Active shopping and become the point of purchase?

Finally, how can I expedite the sale so that the person does not abandon the sale?

This final point is important in all retailers. In a situation where shoppers are time poor, such as airports or in convenience stores, even a short queue at the till will make some abandon the product they have selected and leave.

This behaviour in grocery superstores was the reason that 1 plus 1 queueing systems were developed. The basic idea is that if all tills have one customer waiting and one being served a new till will be opened. This continues until all the tills are open.

In multi category stores these processes will need to be achieved for each category if you wish to maximise basket size and take the maximum share of pocket. It is highly unlikely that we will achieve 100%, although it should be the objective. One of the things that drives retailers crazy is the thought that a shopper is in their store and fails to buy a product that they subsequently buy somewhere else in the next 24 hours at the same price or higher.

Challenges to manufacturers have to include encouraging them to help meet these objectives. The truth is this will become more difficult as retailers, using traditional strategies, become outdated and easily replaced by online shopping. Amazon are already moving into grocery with many others building strategies to follow.

Even manufacturers now have direct access to consumers if they choose to cut out the retailer and go online. The boom of the discounter retailer across Europe may literally go boom! As fast as it has grown due to its simple, price driven strategy it can be outmoded just as quickly by better prices and more choice from the internet.

The key way big brand manufacturers will support retail is if the stores provide benefits not replicable by online and also help build loyalty with their consumers.

But it will not be as easy for Brands in the future. I mentioned Dan Herman earlier and he has a particular perspective on this. He is a great advocate of encouraging Brands to deliver off core benefits to consumers as well as the traditional ones associated with their product. By off core he means attributes which are, not only at odds or not associated with a products actual use, but also unlikely to be copied by other manufacturers.

He uses the example of Virgin Atlantic whose unorthodox approach to advertising and challenging the status quo provides customers with the chance to have fun in a typically serious environment. They do not focus on core benefits such as the leg room and size of the TV in business. For Virgin it is more important to be the cool, naughty kid that gets in the face of the big, traditional guys. Google their advert "flying in the face of ordinary". They are so un P.C. but they make you smile. Their planes reflect this by having bars on board (often seen with James Bond sitting at them drinking a Vesper) and even offer massages.

To help isolate opportunities Dr Herman abandons typical segmentation strategies and focus at building Long Term Brands. He uses a system called "O-Scan" to highlight opportunities and "ForeSearch" to discover potential desires in consumers.

Both systems offer the chance to uncover sustainable competitive advantages for manufacturers. These off core approaches are ideally suited to help provide retailers a point of difference which will allow them to compete with e-tailing.

Without this we will have very few alternatives for the future.

Currently, retail strategies being planned by some of the multinationals, go in two distinctly opposite directions.

Strategy one, how can I remain a retailer and not have any stores?

Strategy two, how can I benefit customers in ways that the internet and my competitors cannot replicate.

Believe it or not strategy one is beginning to happen for some already. Potential write down of bricks and mortar assets are being considered along with plans to downsize store size and numbers.

These decisions are not being taken based on the best interests of society or employees. As always self interest steps in to make certain survival, in any form, is better than eradication.

So why should we, as individual members of society, care if bricks and mortar downsizes on mass and within a relatively short space of time. Well for several reasons.

Since ancient civilisation, society has built up around trading locations all over the globe. Carthage, Nassau, Genoa, London, Singapore, Hong Kong, Ephesus all grew because of the trade that took place there.

Cities and towns all over the world thrive when commerce goes well. The opposite also applies. No or low levels of retailing in local areas will have a significant effect. First and foremost on the staff of these stores. No store, no staff.

Secondly with manufacturers. No need for a field team if the field is empty apart from a few sheep and lots of logistics vehicles. The same goes for Finance, HR, Marketing. You get the picture.

Other retail support businesses will also suffer. How many Category Management or Merchandising companies realise the potential risks they face. It is unlikely the boom in logistics will take up the slack so there will be a net loss.

Finally there will be a social impact. Enough of the stores will disappear to create a shift in the physical structure of neighbourhoods. I am not talking about every store closing but, with a relatively small shift to the internet, it will be enough to make locations unviable on a balance sheet. The companies who will do well will be the ones printing Closed signs.

It is easy to think traditionally, respond to the market pressures, and take your business online completely. Follow the trend is the common sense approach because you can't fight the tide.

So everybody ends up with a me too offer online now. Genius! That will protect the business from its current fragility won't it?

Look around your place of work at the Leaders driving your business. How many of them are actually Followers not Leaders? Do they have the metal to take on a real challenge or would they prefer to follow a trend, even if it is a bad one? Perhaps it's you not them that can make the change.

For real business Leaders there could be another option.
What if you say "screw the trend. I don't like it and I don't like what it means to my business, the people around me and society in general. It's ugly, unexciting and wrong. In fact I am going to make my own trend!"

That would be real Leadership.

What if we can re-ignite retail. Make it so damn fun, exciting and sexy people will queue for miles. A&F can do it, why cant we? Have you ever seen Saks Fifth Avenue when its at full speed?

Retail Shopper Management has to now take shape and become part of strategy two. Strategy two is not going to be delivered by Category Management. Category Management may be partly responsible for creating the dangerous fragility inherent in many major FMCG companies and other retailers. It may not have been murder after all. Category Management may have seen what it was doing to retail and decided to fall on its sword.

As an ex retailer I cannot be unbiased. I want bricks and mortar to continue, strengthen and grow. Done well, it is not only highly profitable, it is great fun for everyone and creates communities where we can socialise.

A great example of this is Town Square in Las Vegas. An edge of city community where people shop, socialise, live, eat and play interspersed with good retailers. If you have the opportunity try spending an evening there and take your kids. If they are under 10 they will beg to go back. Its a start but so much more can be done. http://www.mytownsquarelasvegas.com

So that being the case, how can we start to understand the metrics of retailing and manufacturing in more detail? Where should we focus our attention to gain maximum benefit?

I offer this framework to help and it expands on the traditional model of more, to more people, more often. It also draws from the stages a person goes through on the way to a purchase decision, as mentioned above.

It will help dissect store and product offerings to assist in understanding where the issues lay and where the opportunities are.

Many enlightened people have talked about the importance of finding the right questions so I would like to quote from the wisest of all. Kwai Chang Caine from the TV series Kung Fu. He once said "I seek not to know the answers, but to understand the questions".

Populate the following table with data and the right questions will appear. If you ask the right question you stand a chance of getting the correct answer.

So here comes the technical bit. It will be a bit dry to start off with and some of it may be quite obvious and common sense. Good. I like simple, elegant and common sense. There is far too much spin being put on simple ideas. If it is pure and it works it is probably a more useful solution than the most complicated, jargon filled drivel we are often treated to.

Read Jony Ive on the subject.

The good news is that many of you will discover opportunities to make millions of dollars if you get it right.

Even a salesperson calling on a corner shop will find opportunities for their customer if they can adapt the idea to that location.

This version is focused at retailers but it is easy to use an adapted version to analyse a manufacturers products as well. It is not definitive but meant as a guide.

	Consumption	Purchase in all Locally Related Stores vs this Store	Visit to all Locally Related Stores vs this Store	Consideration	Opportunity
More **Weight**	Average serving (Unit)	Average volume of purchase per visit in this store vs average volume bought across all local retailers annually	Volume bought in this retailer on each visit vs actual purchase weight in similar stores local	Volume of product 1 person can consume if 0% of similar substitutionary products are cannibalised e.g. volume a person who eats take out meals would consume if they cooked instead	Total volume opportunity for that store minus actual sales
More Often **Frequency**	Number of consumption events	Number of purchase events annually in this store vs number of events in similar types of stores annually	Number of visits to similar types of local stores annually vs this store	% of times a retailer is considered as a point of purchase for this event vs all local competitors	Total number of potential purchase events for that store minus actual events
More People **Penetration**	% of People consuming annually	% of shoppers purchasing in this store vs population purchasing locally	% of visits to this retailer annually vs total local market shopping relevant categories	% of people who consider this retailer as a point of purchase vs all local competitors	Number of people able to shop this store geographically if consideration is 100% minus the actual number

So the idea of more, to more, more often is then broken down over five levels.

Consumption, Purchase, Visit, Consideration and Opportunity.

Consumption does what it says on the tin.
Purchase in all locally related stores
Purchase in this store
Visit in all locally related stores
Visit in this store
Consideration of all locally related stores and each category within store
Consideration of this store and each category within store
Opportunity total size or mass of local market based on 100% consideration minus actuals

As you begin to fill in this sheet the natural equations highlighting a significant dollar upside will appear before your eyes.   Not only that but it will be easy to see where to target first.

Each of these offers the chance for retailers and manufacturers to understand where significant opportunity gaps are.   We can even integrate lost sales to e-tail.

If you are an Account Manager visiting a convenience store and do not have access to this level of information you can make some good assumptions just by counting shoppers passing the store vs entering vs buying each category.   That and a little market information will give you an insight.

If you have the resources of a major corporation it becomes easier.

Run this against a retail chain or manufacturers products within a store and you will gain clarity as to where the problem or opportunity lays.

It takes a while to create the data but, when it is done, you can use it to help measure how initiatives are affecting these metrics. Finding the opportunity gaps, and believe me this model will uncover immense dollar value for many of you, is not the big deal.   Finding gaps has been around for thousands of years. What is important is thinking differently about the solution.

As soon as you get this value insight the real fun starts. Now you can start the process of integrating store data and consumer insight to, not only understand the causes of the problem, but begin the process of filling the gap in an innovative way.

It's not just about using traditional insights it's about emotional insights.

And I will give you a hint. If your answer depends on price, value or range as opposed to includes price, value and range your competitors will catch you in a month.

If you use off core benefits for products and emotional added value reasons to shop this store, your competitors will spend their lives playing catch up. Especially if you make it part of your culture.

Focus on meeting peoples desires not just their needs. Most needs are being catered for now. Either by you or your competitors. Try to meet these existing needs in a more exciting way that helps fulfil peoples fantasies.

Low level impact is delivered by satisfying **needs**. Traditional marketing methods have fulfilled them in most developed markets.
Advanced thinking satisfies **desires** which are more difficult to discover.
High level impact is achieved when you complete the others but can also fulfil deep seated **fantasies**.

Fantasies are the fuel of life. Most people only get as far as realising some of their dreams. Help fulfil a fantasy and you are in a different league.

I can use a simple example in the movie world that has been massively successful for over 50 years. When the latest James Bond movie is released it works on multiple levels. It satisfies a need for entertainment and social interaction. It goes further by meeting a desire to be excited, shocked, thrilled. Finally and most powerfully it allows every man in the theatre to live the life that fills their fantasies.

Someone capable, in control, resourceful, sexually in demand and powerful. For many women in the audience they see the bad guy they always secretly wanted to sweep them off their feet and they mentally become the Bond girl who he saves.

This is a slight (ok huge) generalisation and does not describe everyone but it does describe enough for the franchise to sustain itself and grow over decades. If you want to test my observations wait for the next release and watch the audience as they leave the theatre. Men walk more confidently and have adrenalin fuelled tension in their muscles. Women leave in one of a couple of frames of mind. They either see those characteristics in the man they are with and hold him close or they have a distance between them as she thinks "where did my life go so wrong?"

James Bond movies tend to be released at the end of November. Guess when my son James birthday is? Yes I am that easily sucked into my own fantasies given the chance.

Any behavioural analyst worth their salt will tell you it's fatal for anyone to draw conclusions when they map their own personality across the sample but sometimes you have to accept you are also part of the sample. Using common sense and good observation of people is a tremendous skill. If we are not genuinely interested in the why of people's behaviour in addition to the what we will fail to uncover their real motivations.

Dan Herman's team run consumer interviews that can last over an hour and are facilitated by a highly skilled crew. Only through this technique can they get to the real desires people have.

There is also an old technique called the seven fold why. After asking why seven times you are normally at the heart of the problem and dealing with the truth not a symptom. I believe it comes from the fact that it is virtually impossible to fold a piece of normal paper more than seven times. That's the limit.

Try it. It`s simple and it may work for you when talking to shoppers.

At the beginning of this book we started with a murder. It is now time to find out the facts behind what happened. We need to understand the motives and importantly who the assassin was.

Lets raise the curtain on our final act.

10 WHO KILLED CATEGORY MANAGEMENT?
OR
"WHY DOES EVERYONE THINK I AM A MERCHANT BANKER?"

In 1762 two brothers, John and Francis, found themselves in London starting their own business. It was imaginatively called the John and Francis Baring Company. Most people knew it simply as Barings Bank.

The boys had began one of the longest standing merchant banks in the world. It evolved over two centuries as a home for international investment and grew way beyond its humble beginnings in Cheapside.

By 1995 it had international offices one of which was located in Singapore close to the historical Boat Quay area of the city. The architecture of the area is extraordinary. Two story buildings echoing its beginnings in 1842 are set beneath a backdrop of skyscrapers which showcase its 21st century commercial standing.

Facing out onto the Singapore River, in one of the old low rise structures, is a bar called Harrys. Harrys close geographic location to the financial district meant it was a watering hole for many of the traders. In 1995 one of those was Nick Leeson.

Nick was one of Barings stars and personally accounted for a large percentage of their profits. That came to an end very abruptly. His trading gambled on the future of the Japanese markets. This collapsed after the Kobe earthquake sent Asia into free fall.

Losses totalling $1.3 Billion mounted fast and when it was eventually discovered it triggered the failure of one of the oldest and most respected banks on the planet.

This was the first time a serious bank had failed so publicly in the modern era. It signalled to investors that banks were as fragile as most other types of business.

When Lehman Brothers collapsed thirteen years later it triggered a world wide banking crisis that still has repercussions today.

Faith in large organisations and their stock value are largely based on confidence. While trading is going well these multinational businesses seem bullet proof and attract significant investment.

Currently that is happening with most large scale retailers. The issue is that confidence can collapse in weeks or days and, like a house of cards, come crashing down around us.

This is where some retailers sit today. Financially secure as long as the confidence remains high but as fragile as the banks when the world sees them for what they are.

The news tonight is filled by Amazon. It has unveiled plans for Prime Air. A flying drone system that can carry packages up to five pounds (this covers about 86% of Amazon orders) for a radius of 10 miles.

Parcels delivered in 30 minutes or less by a fleet of flying, unmanned couriers that wait at the end of a conveyor ready to fulfil your online purchase.

Yes this is very pie in the sky for FMCG at the moment (excuse the pun) and has many hurdles in front of it before it will become reality. But the momentum has started.

How many more Prime Air initiatives will it take to shatter the fragility of traditional retailing? The clock is ticking as the first cracks start to appear in that retail confidence house of glass.

So lets answer our original question, who killed Category Management?

Well we have to understand who could benefit from its demise. There is only one real winner if Category Management dies in its current form. Retail.

Retail has a childlike innocence. It is the product of its parents. Good parents will produce a healthy well balanced child that can integrate with the requirements of society and add value to them. A healthy member of a flourishing group. Bad parents will produce a dysfunctional child unable to cope with social demands and at odds with the world around it. A business at best able to rage against itself and everyone around it until it breaks down.

Retails parents are not fictional. They are us. They are the people around you, both within manufacturers and in the retailing companies themselves. If we need to understand who will be responsible for the demise of retail on the high street it will be us through our low level ambition, fear of risk and an inability to drive change within our companies.

If it is to survive, the future of retail will be forged in the furnace of revolutionary change. Very few realise the fragile structure of the chains that surround us.

Over decades national and international retailers have been responsible for the demise of independent, unique shopping experiences.

Now it is their turn to be put on the endangered species list. Size does not equal success or security anymore.

You will have to be brave or confident that a retailer has the ability to completely re-invent itself if you decide to invest in them.

It is the same fantasy land the banking system found itself in. When one person realises the king is not wearing any clothes it will create a tsunami of failure.

The business model in grocery, electronics, fashion, home furnishings, DIY and many others will not weather this storm if they remain in their current incarnation.

Who killed Category Management?

The truth is if you are in major retail or manufacturing. It was probably you. In the library. With the candlestick. Relying on it so heavily, just because it has worked well for years, meant you put it firmly in the cross hairs of an assassins rifle.

Its success was hiding its inherent failure.

But here is the great thing. Maybe it needed killing. Perhaps you are one of the handful of people that will be first to raise the bar.

Once raised everybody else has to follow or or die.

To everyone involved in Category Management here is the opportunity we need to create a point of difference and develop a sustainable competitive edge.

Integrate its old strengths into a wider view of the shopper. Raise your ambition for what part you play in peoples lives and deliver on the promise of satisfying not only a customers needs but their desires and fantasies. Make them feel, allow them to experience emotion in stores and encourage them to see retail as an experience not a service.

Its up to you. You decide on the how the next chapter for retailing ends. Is it the prologue of a new beginning or the epilogue to a fine story.

Thank you for reading the book and humouring my bad jokes and gross generalisations. I hope that you have been angered by some of it, laughed at other parts and, in my wildest dreams, inspired to be a little different tomorrow.

ABOUT THE AUTHOR

Mark has spent his life in commercial FMCG roles both in Manufacturing and Retail. More recently he also specialised in people development including Leadership programs.

During his career he acknowledges he has been very lucky to have worked with some exceptional professionals who have helped shape his life.

These have helped him enjoy success across diverse industries including Alcohol, Fashion, Electrical, Confectionary, Grocery, Tobacco, I.T. plus many others.

He specialises in negotiation, sales, buying, commercial strategy, marketing and teaching but he holds a special place in his heart for boat rocking with a smattering of tree shaking.

He now spends his time working with organisations that want to move their people, business and commercial results foreword by delivering something really special for their customers.

As you will notice from the book, his style is very straight forward and he values partnerships that seek the truth, not just a sugar coated pill to massage egos. Life is just too short for that.

An accomplished public speaker he also enjoys key note opportunities. If you need your audience to be challenged to think differently about manufacturing and retail he is guaranteed to create a platform for discussion.

Make some magic happen.

www.whokilledcategorymanagement.com

CPSIA information can be obtained at www.ICGtesting.com
Printed in the USA
LVOW06s1708200715

446912LV00018B/1415/P